Karen Rouse is a newspaper reporter for three publications in northeastern Michigan and learned of Jodi and Mari's inspirational story after interviewing Homaune when she was named "Investigation Discovery's Everyday Hero of the Month" in December 2014. Jodi used the recognition and monetary award to promote the MotherDaughter Fund she and her daughter founded in 2012. The MD fund helps families with research, recovery and reunification of family members who have gone missing.

"Jodi's energy and enthusiasm in helping families is contagious. It is a highlight of my career to help her tell her story of how faith, perseverance, and love really can conquer all, even in the darkest of times."

Acknowledgements

Where do I begin; first I must thank my daughter Mari for believing in her Mom. For being the strong little girl she was at the time of her abduction and for believing that she and I were supposed to be together again.

My very special parents Vern and Marilyn, you have given me a lifetime of love, support and the ability to never give up. Thank you for giving me my faith and most of all believing in me and my abilities to rescue your granddaughter.

To my brothers and their families, there were moments when I thought Mari and I would never see all of you again. I have so many memories of love and laughter with each one of you locked in my heart, that it kept me going in the darkest of days. I will forever be proud of the men my brothers have become.

To the entire Moore and Reed Family, your prayers and thoughts will forever be shared with Mari. To my cousin John Gaedert you will be remembered in my heart forever for what you did for Mari and I to be back together. Your advice about family lives within me.

LeaAnn, Elsie, Liz, Mark, Tom, Dennis, Melissa, Lisa, Ferris, George, Jerry, Susan, Abby and Monty, you define friendship.

Special Agent Robby and Victims Specialist Donna of the FBI- no words can describe what the two of you mean to Mari and me. No one believed more then you that together we could rescue Mari. 802 days it took us to do it and not once during those days did I doubt your abilities and I don't believe you doubted mine. The incredible emotional journey the three of us had will never leave my heart and I thank God every day that you were my agents.

To the many embassies and consulates around the world, F.B.I. Legates, National Center for Missing & Exploited Children and Team Hope, I thank you with all of my heart for being there for Mari and I.

Karen Rouse you are one of the most amazing women I have met in my life and I thank you for bringing our story to words.

I dedicate this book to all the missing children and their families around the world. **Never, ever, ever** give up in the journey to find your children or your loved ones.

Jodi

Dear Reader,

I decided to tell our story because I believe the ultimate betrayal of a parent to his/her child is to take away the child's other parent. Of course there are exceptions to that rule as with everything. *Perfidious* is my daughter's and my journey as we remember it. Dialogue was reconstructed for narrative purposes, but we have done our best to stay true to the conversations, the facts of the events and the relationships portrayed. I am sure everyone involved in our journey may have their own perceptions of the journey.

During the duration of my daughter's abduction it was made clear to me that this was my fault. Not only did the abductor make this very clear, complete strangers threw comments my way that I never saw coming, which made me think my daughter's abduction was my fault.

I wanted so bad to tell them the guilt I was feeling. I wanted them to know that the person I knew for 8 years would never do this. This wasn't some random person that I allowed to take my daughter on a vacation. This was her father. This man had taken us both on vacation. This man laughed with me, cried with me, loved our daughter with me. So yes, in the end it was my fault. I was played and deceived and I didn't see this coming.

After my daughter was missing for over a year I met a woman named Abby Potash. Abby called me one day and said the FBI had given her my name and asked her to reach out to me. Abby was and is the director of a group called Team HOPE of the National Center for Missing and Exploited Children. Team HOPE is a group of ordinary people who one day were forced to live every parent's nightmare. They know the pain, fear, frustration and loneliness that come with having a missing or sexually exploited child. With this knowledge and experience, they offer peer support to families of missing and sexually exploited children.

Abby was the first person outside of the FBI that didn't make me feel that I had caused this to happen to my daughter. She helped me realize that parental abductions happen and sometimes there is no warning.

Parental abductions are still such a strange topic for people to talk about. No one wants to believe it can happen to them. I was 45 years old when my daughter was abducted and up until that time I personally did not know any cases of parental abduction.

Now that it has been a few years since my daughter and I have been back together, I work in the field of locating missing loved ones. The stories of the families I work with are very similar to each other because they are searching for missing loved ones. The cases are heartbreaking in ways you can't imagine. I pray I can be one of many voices to them that never judge the situation that led to their children being abducted or missing.

Read my journey. Laugh at me, cry with me, yell at me, call me stupid and ask me -*what was I thinking*. It is OK; God has given me strength that I could never imagine.

Once I got Mari back to the United States I realized our journey had really just begun. The effect of a parentally abducted child and the steps it takes to get to a "new normal" is an amazing journey. ***Jodi***

P.S.
    Keep your eyes watching for "*The Journey Back to Normal*" A book that will make you laugh and cry as you read about our reunification and finding our lives again.

PERFIDIOUS

Jodi Homaune and Karen Rouse

Copyright © 2016 Jodi Homaune and Karen Rouse
All rights reserved.

ISBN: 1533575096
ISBN 13: 9781533575098
Library of Congress Control Number: 2016911164
CreateSpace Independent Publishing Platform
North Charleston, South Carolina

My Dearest Mari,

You are truly the bravest person I know and I will forever be in awe of you and what you endured to get back home to your Mommy.
    I pray that the journey of your past makes you stronger for all your tomorrows.
    With all my love,
    Mom

CHAPTER 1

AUGUST 7, 2011; MIDDAY
JOHN F. KENNEDY INTERNATIONAL AIRPORT; NEW YORK, NY

JODI HOMAUNE WOULD LATER SAY that she didn't know how she was going to accomplish the rescue of her daughter, but she did. A journey which would take two years and three months, before she would have Mari back in her arms. Eight-hundred and two days before Jodi could bring her daughter's ordeal to an end.

Events beyond her control found her waiting for a connecting flight at John F. Kennedy International Airport to board a plane for Istanbul, Turkey where she alone would be responsible for orchestrating Mari's release back to her mother's custody. The State Department and FBI had made it very clear to her there was little they could do to help during the process of rescuing Mari. It would lie in the hands of Jodi and her Turkish attorney, whom she had yet to meet. Still, Jodi said she felt no fear; only a consuming motherly drive to make sure Mari was safe and loved and back on U.S. soil. She would be traveling across eight time zones and against all odds imaginable to bring her back home.

She wondered if she was the only one among hundreds, no, thousands of people at the airport who were about to do what she was going to do. Was it dangerous? Yes. She even had left notarized documents authorizing her brother Matthew and his wife Nancy to take full physical and legal custody of Mari and to continue the journey to bring her home in case Jodi was killed or if illness claimed her life. She had prayed to God when she had drawn up the documents. She had prayed and begged God that if anything happened to her on her way to Turkey, or while in Turkey, that He would provide her brother Matt with the strength to see that Mari was protected and brought back home to live with him and his wife Nancy.

Mari hadn't deserved any of what had happened and absolutely did not deserve anything less than being in a loving family who adored her. Jodi knew that Matt and Nancy and their two sons would provide this for her. The papers which had been drawn up provided Jodi with a sense of peace once they had been notarized and signed by all parties involved.

She had said goodbye to Matt and his family at Detroit Metro Airport in Michigan. The five of them had spent the week together at the family cabin before her departure, which they had dubbed "Mari Headquarters." It was a difficult goodbye for Matt, because he knew that once his older sister was out of his sight, there was nothing he could do to protect or help her.

Matt had a vision of his sister that she could do anything. She had beaten weird cancers and unusual childhood illnesses and he had grown up watching her play basketball, run track and cheer on anyone who seemed to be having a bad day.

As Jodi wove her way through the security maze, Matt's eyes never left hers. They locked eyes at every turn and his eyes were filled with pain and worry. Jodi mouthed, "I can do this; I will bring Mari home. Take care of Mom and Dad and tell them that I love them."

She could see the tears in her brother's eyes and for a moment, she reflected on him, her baby brother. He had been a college football player, a Golden Gloves champ and had a heart of pure gold. She could sense he was having a hard time letting her get on that plane without him.

As she turned the corner, she had the chance to look over at his wife Nancy and at each of their sons, Luke and Jake. Nancy gave up the best smile she could muster as tears flowed down her cheeks.

Perfidious

Nancy had been a saint the week before Jodi left for Istanbul. She made food and forcibly persuaded Jodi to eat. She packed for Jodi's trip and kept the entire family organized. She had even convinced Jodi to take a box of granola bars with her, just in case she couldn't get food. Jodi loved her sister-in-law; she was the sister Jodi never had.

Luke and Jake looked at their "Aunt Jo" with fear in their faces as they said goodbye. The drama and stress they had experienced the week leading up to her departure was too much for any child to endure, thought Jodi. She felt proud of how they continued to act as strong young gentlemen during the family turmoil.

Jodi took one last glance at all of them and again thought of how much she loved her family and how lucky she was.

Life without Mari had become a very black and white world for Jodi – one void of any color. It was a strange sensation to live in that world, she often thought. As she went through security, it felt like moving in slow motion as she placed her cell phone, purse and briefcase in a gray bin before tossing her sandals into it. She removed her watch and took out her pony tail ribbon – just in case. She shook her hair down and chuckled to herself thinking what would happen if the person at the scanner told her to remove the contents of her briefcase to see what she was carrying.

Her case weighed at least 40 pounds and she wondered what security would think if they saw numerous FBI business cards, other various business cards, notes and legal papers she was carrying with her, all of which were about her missing child.

Mari colored her world. A long-awaited only child, she was born when Jodi was in her late 30s and was welcomed into the world with open arms by not only Jodi, but her father Kevin as well. Jodi marveled at their daughter, with her full head of dark hair and bright alert eyes. Inspecting her newborn as all new mothers have done throughout time, Jodi noticed a mole behind her left ear, almost like a giant freckle.

"Well, that must be the Irish in her," Jodi thought.

Their beautiful daughter was half Irish and half Iranian. As a newborn, she looked like she had received the best from both her parents, which made Jodi extremely happy. Mari was healthy, thriving and simply amazing. She had been born two months premature and weighed only three pounds at birth.

Naming her daughter after both of her grandmothers gave Jodi such joy. Here she was world - - -Mari Batool! Her first name was after her American grandmother Marilyn, Jodi's mother, and her middle name was after her Iranian grandmother Batool, Kevin's mother.

Jodi didn't feel her normal energetic curiosity about flying to Istanbul. The thought never crossed her mind about how far she was traveling, the area she was traveling to and if it was dangerous. Instead, she was trying to remember all of the details she had memorized to prepare for the unknown. She ran Farsi sentences through her head in case Mari would now be speaking Farsi, or if she would feel more comfortable speaking Farsi instead of English. She practiced Turkish phrases and sentences because she knew she would need them while in Turkey. She could see the maps of Turkey and the surrounding areas in her head, confident she knew the layout of Istanbul like the back of her hand.

Millions and millions of thoughts kept flashing through her head and she knew it was time; time to let go of her family and worrying about her parents; time to let go of thoughts of her brothers and their families and all the worries related to loving people so much. She knew she had to focus on just one thing only - her job of getting Mari safely back home.

She had made herself a promise that once she got through security, she would forget about everyone else and focus on becoming the mother God had intended her to be. The one that was willing to do anything, and face anything to rescue her daughter out of Turkey. The thought gave Jodi a feeling she called "Mommy Power." She had grown to love the sensation over the past two years and three months. She had counted on that energy in her darkest days without Mari. It saved her from falling into a dark place she was sure she would not have been able to get out of. "Mommy Power" came from her faith and she truly believed the energy came straight from God.

CHAPTER 2

August 7, 2011
JFK Airport; New York

JODI (REED) GREW UP IN Hale, a small Michigan town surrounded by her immediate family and a community filled with friends. It was the type of town where people looked out for one another, cared about each other and cheered each other on in the best and worst of times. An all-American life is what Jodi knew she had, with a stay-at-home mother who was creative and artistic and a father who was a teacher and the head football coach of her high school.

With their mother's artistic and musical abilities and their father's athletic abilities, the Reed children had the best of both worlds. Their home was filled with music, sports and a strong faith. Early on, the Reed children learned that it was their goal in life to give more to the world than they took from it. Jodi was taught when she started something, she would be expected to finish it to the best of her ability. If someone needed anything, her family did everything in their power to see that they got it.

The Reed home was filled with love, faith and character building experiences. Being the only daughter and the middle child, Jodi grew up strong and independent and was known as the peace maker in their tight family.

Making it through security, she guessed no one was curious about the stuff packed in her brief case, which was fine with her. She tied her white sweater around her waist, pulled her hair back up in a ponytail and flipped on her sandals. Jodi had chosen to wear a tan sun dress she had worn for years. It was simple, very comfortable and she knew the weather would be quite warm when she arrived in Istanbul.

Most of Jodi's girlfriends would have shuddered at her outfit, she knew, as she thought about the style she called her own. She grew up a tomboy, so fashion wasn't a priority in her life and it sometimes showed. Her best days were spent wearing a pair of jeans, white sneakers and a tunic T-shirt that had seen better days. When she found a pair of earrings she liked, usually little pearls, or small gem pieces, she wore them forever and usually forgot to change them until one of her friends would make a comment to her about it. Jodi's taste in clothes was simple and she could easily take three or four pieces to make up outfits which she thought looked respectable.

Pulling herself together after going through security, she looked for the first place to get a sandwich and hot tea. Jodi had made a promise to Donna, an FBI victim's specialist assigned to her that she would eat at the airport to keep her strength up. She would have much to do when she arrived in Istanbul. She also recalled Robby, her FBI agent, telling her to rest while on the flight to Istanbul, because she would need to "hit the ground running."

Robby and Donna had become very important people in Jodi's life. There were days when she would feel that no one could ever understand what she and Mari were living with; the pain, the unknown and comments people made holding Jodi responsible for what happened to her daughter. Some days, it was too much to bear or hear and Robby and Donna had become her lifeline – her connection to humanity, as they would listen to Jodi's rants and rambles.

Daily phone calls to her parents were her connection to reality, which helped Jodi hold on to her belief that she would see Mari again. They became a symbol to Jodi that life would return to normal one day.

At the airport Jodi's mind was so active that it was almost impossible to eat or rest. She was expecting a call from the State Department in

Turkey, from the people who were with Mari. Jodi had been told that she would be able to speak with her daughter while she was in New York waiting for her connecting flight. The memory of Mari's voice from a conversation the night before replayed in her head. It was the first time mother and daughter had spoken with each other in more than two years without Mari's father telling them both what to say. When the call came through, Jodi knew immediately that Mari was weary and frightened. Jodi thought Mari sounded like a four-year-old, instead of an eight-year-old, which worried her. It tore at her soul to know that Mari was so scared.

"Mari, I need you to listen to me and pay very close attention. Can you do that for Mommy, sweetie?"

"Yes, I will Mommy," Mari said in a quiet voice. "Where am I going? Will you find me?"

"Mari," Jodi said as confidently as she could sound. "Lisa is going to take you to a building where you will be very safe. I will come to you there." Jodi didn't want to say orphanage, because as much as it scared Jodi to say it, she knew it would frighten Mari more if she understood the word.

"There are other little girls to play with, so you will have fun." As Jodi was saying this, she hoped with all her heart this was true. Mari was speaking with a heavy Iranian accent and Jodi could tell she had to try and remember English as she struggled with some of her words.

"Will Baba be able to get me there?" Mari asked, obviously worrying about her father.

As Jodi heard those words, it brought her to that dark place she had been in for more than two years. Her eyes filled with tears, yet she knew she had to stay strong for Mari, as she fought against her fear of the unknown. What had happened to her daughter? Was she loved? Had someone comforted Mari when she cried?

"No, sweetie, you are safe and will stay that way until Mommy comes to get you. Mari can you blow me a kiss? I need one really bad . . ." A second passed before Mari blew her mother a kiss over the phone.

"I caught it and rubbed it all over my face," Jodi giggled to Mari and then said, "Here comes a magic one for you Mari, catch it!"

"I caught it, Mommy." The lack of enthusiasm in Mari's voice shocked Jodi, yet she knew her daughter had been through so much during the previous 48 hours, that it wasn't a surprise how she sounded. They said their "I love you's, and with the promise from Jodi that she would be there soon, Mari handed the phone back to Lisa, the woman from the State Department.

Lisa quickly told Jodi that Mari was doing OK. Physically, she appeared fine - the doctors at the hospital had checked her out and said as much. Lisa went on to explain that Mari's eye sight concerned them and that she was having a difficult time seeing clearly. Her eyes would need attention once she got home; however, the doctors said her blurry vision might be from being upset and crying so much the last few days. She told Jodi that Mari was still crying and having a hard time stopping.

Jodi thought her heart was going to break and could physically feel it pounding in her chest. Lisa explained Mari had been through so much but seemed to perk up when she heard Jodi's voice. She went on to say that they were taking her to the orphanage right after the doctor was done with his examination and the police were finished talking with her.

"Wait a second; Mari wants to talk to you again." Lisa handed Mari the phone.

"Mommy, can you bring Junior with you? I want to see him so bad," Mari said, pleading. Jodi could imagine her daughter's eyes dancing as she asked the question. Junior was Mari's pet frog. She had found him the second weekend they arrived in Virginia in 2007 and he was her beloved friend. He slept in Mari's room, rode on her bicycle with her and rode on Mari's toy train every day. Early on, Kevin had forbidden Jodi to talk about Junior with Mari. He made it very clear that there would be no discussion about Mari's frog, no discussions about her life in America, no discussions about her grandparents, her friends, school and absolutely no discussions about Mari returning home.

Later on, Jodi would find out that Mari was not allowed to ever talk about those things with anyone in Iran. Not about her mother, her grandparents, her family, her life or her memories.

She explained to Mari that as much as she wanted to bring Junior, he didn't have a ticket to fly this time.

"But, Mommy just put him in your pocket and bring him. He will behave – I promise!" Mari was again pleading and at that moment Jodi knew that everything was going to be OK.

"I promise Sweetie. Junior will be here when you get home. Now go with Lisa and I will see you soon."

The round of, "I love you's," were repeated. For the first time in more than two years, Jodi felt like she had talked with the Mari she knew so well and loved so much. Jodi tried to put what Lisa said about Mari's eyes in the back of her mind. What she needed to focus on was just getting to Turkey and getting her home.

Jodi placed the phone in her lap and just stared at it for a moment - fully enjoying the excitement of hearing Mari asking about Junior. A smile was forming across her face. Was their nightmare about to end?

Somewhere to the right of where she was sitting she heard someone ask if she was flying to Istanbul. Jodi looked up and straight in to the eyes of a very stylish, yet more mature woman who was smiling directly at her. The woman looked so put together. Blonde, with her hair pulled up in a ponytail, like Jodi was wearing, yet the woman was stunning in her matching outfit, which matched her bags, which also matched her shoes. Jodi noticed the woman's sculptured nails, khaki pants topped with a little jean jacket and bottled water packed neatly in the side of her traveling bag. Jodi thought she must be very well-traveled and sophisticated.

For a second, Jodi just stared at her; she didn't feel like or have time for idle chit-chat. She had promised Robby her FBI Agent, that she would call him right after she got her call from Mari.

Jodi first thought was to pretend she didn't understand English, but she didn't know if the woman had heard her conversation with Mari.

"Yes, I am traveling to Istanbul," Jodi politely answered. She hoped that would satisfy the woman and she could go back to her thoughts of Mari.

"On vacation?" the woman smiled, seeming to want to generate conversation.

"No, I am going to pick up my daughter." As the words rolled out of her mouth, it took Jodi by surprise to be able to finally say them. She wasn't accustomed to talking about Mari with strangers and it made her uncomfortable.

The woman persisted with her questions and with a surge of energy said, "Oh, so she is in college... I just think it is so great that students can study abroad. What is she majoring in? Diplomacy? Cultural history? Oh! Its archaeology isn't it?" The woman became more and more animated, excited that she had found someone to talk with. She continued the one-sided conversation with Jodi.

"Blah, blah, blah," the words floated over Jodi like cartoon balloons. She couldn't process what the friendly stranger was saying as she kept on talking. It seemed to Jodi the woman was Charlie Brown's teacher and she was Charlie Brown. "Wah, Wah, Wah, Wah!"

"No, she isn't in college," Jodi politely said. Had she aged that much in over two years that this woman thought she had a college-aged daughter? She chuckled at the thought. Jodi was normally outgoing and loved to meet new people but she just did not want to have this conversation.

"Did you adopt a girl from Turkey? The woman asked excitedly. Before she could work up an answer the woman started telling Jodi that her friend had adopted a child from another country. Jodi could not remember what the woman said after that; "Charlie Brown's" teacher was talking again. She was anxious to call Robby, but didn't want to be interrupted by this woman, so she blurted out, "My daughter was held in Iran for two years and three months by her father and I am on my way to Istanbul to rescue her out of an orphanage."

Jodi's relief at telling her the truth was over shadowed by how bad she felt as she watched this very energetic woman age before her eyes as she processed what had just been said.

"Oh-my-God," said the woman slowly, increasingly subdued. Right then, Robby texted Jodi and asked her to give him a call. Jodi was very relieved to be out of this conversation and politely told the stranger that she had to call her FBI agent. "I'm sorry, it's important." Jodi gathered her things, proceeded to make the call and then find another place to sit where no one was around.

CHAPTER 3

May 28, 2009
Charlottesville, VA

"Mommy, are you sure you'll take care of Junior?" Mari asked her mom for what felt to her like the 48th time. The diminutive six year old's greenish brown eyes were shining, her long dark hair hanging loose as she was cupping her pet frog in her hands and stroking its head.

Jodi looked up after tucking one of Mari's *National Geographic* magazines into her daughter's suitcase and said, "I promise. Now you have to promise me you'll enjoy going with your Baba to visit your grandparents in Iran."

Mari had slept with Jodi in her bed the night before she left. It was something they did on the weekends after watching movies and eating popcorn; but Jodi wanted the mid-week Wednesday night to be a special memory. After all, Mari would be gone for six weeks.

The featured movie that night included a collection of Tom and Jerry cartoons, Mari's favorite video. Jodi relished and often thought about her daughters developing sense of humor.

Mari had seemed to be born laughing and delighted in making others laugh too. Beginning when she was just two-years-old she would take something out of a bag of groceries, usually vegetables, and hide it under her pillow to tease her mama.

"What happened to our lettuce?" Jodi would ask, and Mari would giggle and say, "I don't know Mama, I just don't know!" Jodi would then pretend that the lettuce walked away and would have the serious responsibility of having to find it.

"Don't look under my pillow... it is not there Mama," Mari would squeal. Then mother and daughter would run to Mari's room and fall on the floor giggling after Jodi pulled the lettuce out from underneath her pillow. Mari would do that every time that they brought groceries home and delighted in the fun game.

After the movie, Jodi and Mari snuggled under the comforter, their heads sinking down into fluffy pillows. Mari looked so small to Jodi in the big bed. Her eyes sparkled as she continued to talk about her family in Iran. She chattered on and on wondering what her grandparents would be like. Would her cousins want to play with her? What games did they know? Did they watch videos? She was taking *Tom and Jerry* on the plane with her to show them. Did they have a VCR? Jodi assured her she could watch the movie on her dad's computer.

She was so excited to meet her aunts and uncles, too. For years her father had told her all about her Iranian family. Jodi and Mari had shared their excitement whenever letters and packages would arrive from Iran.

The gifts would always amaze Jodi; especially the food, candies and nuts. She knew they had to cost a lot of money to send and the family was very generous with their gifts for Mari and herself. She marveled at how much love they showed them through their phone calls and letters.

Grandpa Gazanphar, who had been a great soldier in the Iranian Army, once owned a circus and performed acrobatics when he was younger. Mari knew her grandfather enjoyed drinking Coca-Cola and enjoyed working out to keep fit. She knew that he loved having an American granddaughter and that she was his youngest grandchild. Grandma Batool loved children and was the best cook ever. She had sung to Mari on the phone since the time Mari was a young baby and it delighted Jodi to hear her do that for her granddaughter.

Mari's many aunts showered her with gifts, as well, and Mari could name them all, including how old they were.

As she listened to her daughter and answered her many questions over and over and over, she smiled as she realized sleep would be long in coming that night for both of them.

All too soon, mother and daughter awoke to sunshine and a warm breeze coming in through the open windows. The month of May in Charlottesville, VA was beautiful. It was a perfect day, Jodi remembered. Kevin would be arriving that morning, driving down from Montreal and leaving his BMW at Jodi's home. Jodi would be driving them on the two-hour drive to Dulles International Airport, near Washington D.C.

Mari was excited to see her father and to spend time on an airplane. Only two weeks prior, Mari and Jodi had met Kevin at an Olive Garden in Fredericksburg. Kevin was driving through the area on business and the little family met to talk about the upcoming trip to Iran. As excited as Mari appeared to be about the trip, Jodi knew their little girl was anxious about the separation, never having been apart from her mother for more than eight days.

Jodi had originally planned to accompany Kevin and Mari to Iran, but due to health problems, her plans had to be changed. Jodi would remain in the U.S. and after Kevin and Mari returned, Kevin would stay with them for six weeks, so Jodi could have throat surgery. Kevin would take care of her during her recovery and get Mari off to school each day. He would also help around the house with lifting things and keeping up with their daughter, who possessed an endless amount of energy.

Jodi had just finished taking nine months of a topical onsite chemo for skin cancer on her leg and arm. After surgery, the doctors discovered they had not gotten all of the cancer, and were sure that this chemo treatment would get the rest. The treatment had left some ugly scars on her arm and leg and she had felt like she had the flu for nine months, but everyone believed it had worked. Jodi was run down, but feeling great that she could rest while Mari was on vacation with her father. She felt she would be ready for the surgery on her throat.

When she was 19, her doctor discovered cancerous nodules on her thyroid which were removed. The surgery had removed all of the bad areas and she had the remaining left side of her thyroid intact. Her left side now had multiple nodules and it was recommended that she have those nodules removed. Tests still needed to be performed, but it looked like the surgery was a go when Mari and Kevin were scheduled to return.

Jodi had been exposed to radiation while developing in her mother's womb. Multiple physicians suspected that to be the cause of Jodi's unusual cancers which she has fought since she was a young woman.

While they were meeting in Fredericksburg, Jodi told Kevin of Mari's concerns about being separated from her. "I'm sure its normal for a six year old to feel that way," Jodi said.

Kevin reassured Mari by saying she could call her mother every day and talk on the computer via Skype. He promised to bring her back home, because no mommy and daughter were happier together than the two of them. Jodi was very proud of the way Kevin reassured their daughter and she knew that Kevin loved their little girl. From the time she was born, he adored her and had never before failed her as a father.

Kevin and Jodi had stayed, what some would consider best friends, even after they separated shortly after Mari was born. They both wanted what was best for their daughter and she was their world. When Mari would go away for the weekend with her father, Kevin would allow Mari to call Jodi as much as she wanted. Sometimes Jodi would receive as many as eight phone calls a day, just so Mari could let her mother know she was having fun and that she loved her. Mari's father seemed to enjoy watching his daughter talk with her mother and how they shared things only a mother and daughter could share.

After her father reassured her that she would be able to keep in touch with her mommy every day, Mari's mind seemed to have eased. For the next two weeks the child was eagerly anticipating the father-daughter trip.

Kevin arrived at Jodi and Mari's home on the morning of May 29th, a Thursday. When he drove in, the excitement of seeing him, mingled with the anticipation of the journey, added to the happy atmosphere that Jodi felt. Hugs were given all around before Kevin handed Jodi the keys to his car and unloaded some of his belongings into the house for when he would be back to stay.

As Jodi drove Kevin and Mari to the airport, she enjoyed watching them sit in the back seat and play games. Kevin was teasing Mari that she better grow up to be as pretty as her mommy. Jodi chuckled at his words as she knew she was not Kevin's type of woman and it made it easy for them to get along. Kevin continued on with his teasing.

"Jojo, you look good, I am glad you are done with your treatments on your arm and leg. Don't get too good looking while we are gone, I will have to fight off the men when we get back from Iran," Kevin teased.

As Mari and her father played "I Spy," Jodi chuckled to herself thinking Mari's father would always be a player. Jodi always knew that Kevin loved women. He adored them, the simpler and the needier, the better - especially the very feminine acting ones.

He used to tell Jodi that she didn't need a man like him, because she was strong and independent. Jodi suspected Kevin would always think that the next woman in his life would be just a little bit better than the last; the grass is always greener kind of thing.

Jodi knew he was charming around women. A certain type of charm came out when he was with a member of the opposite sex. It wasn't as obvious as flirting, but a subtle way he had to make a woman feel that she was the only object of his affection. As a woman would walk by, Kevin would make no pretense about checking her out from the corner of his eye. If a woman needed rescuing, Kevin would make himself available. He liked it when Jodi teased him about that part of his personality.

During the ride to the airport, Kevin provided Jodi with a list of names of his family members and phone numbers she didn't already have, just in case they were sightseeing in Iran, she would be able to reach Mari.

Jodi parked her car at the airport and the three of them rolled suitcases into the terminal. Mari was laughing and giggling about riding on a big airplane all the way to Iran. They walked until they had to separate and Jodi recalled it as being such a happy memory. She was excited for

Mari to go on this trip, knowing she was old enough to remember it. When it came time to say goodbye, Jodi was sad because she would miss her daughter while she was gone, but Mari's joy overrode Jodi's sadness.

Mari hugged her mother while giving her kisses and saying she would call her soon. Kevin gave Jodi the giant bear hug she knew so well and he kissed her on the cheek.

"Don't worry Jojo, I will have her call every time she wants," Kevin said. Jodi did not doubt his promise.

Jodi looked up at Kevin and saw tears in his eyes. "Thank you for letting her come with me to visit my family. I only wish you could have been able to come. Next year we will go together, I promise," Kevin whispered.

"Absolutely," Jodi responded, tightening her squeeze in approval.

After Kevin and Mari went through security, Jodi saw Kevin picking Mari up so she could blow kisses and wave goodbye as they walked away.

Kevin looked back at Jodi. At the time, Jodi said she thought it was an odd expression on his face because he could sense how sad she was, but years later Jodi said the look was one that must have been saying good bye.

Jodi's phone rang before she even pulled out of the parking lot at Dulles. Still teary, she answered and tried to sound cheerful. It was Mari calling from the plane. Her little chatterbox had called to tell her how big the plane was and that she was sitting by a window.

"I'll tell you all about my flying and Iran when I get there," Mari said. Mari's voice was filled with childlike wonder as she was about to embark on the biggest adventure of her young life.

Mari's voice floated away and was replaced by Kevin's voice asking if Jodi was OK. She said she was and asked him to give their daughter a squeeze from her and to have a safe flight.

"I will call you when we land in Iran, Jojo. Get some rest," Kevin told Jodi as she buckled up to begin the two-hour drive back to Charlottesville.

CHAPTER 4

July 2009
Charlottesville, VA
(Mari's not coming back)

MARI AND KEVIN WERE DUE back in the states on July 9. Jodi looked at their flight itinerary again and tried to convince herself that Mari would soon be home.

But something was wrong, she didn't know what or why, but it was. Telephone conversations were frequent and regular, yet Kevin had started talking about having problems with Mari's passport and said that he needed her birth certificate mailed to him in Tehran. He assured Jodi that if they couldn't fly to the United States on July 9, he would make sure they would show up before the start of school in the middle of August.

Jodi called Kevin and told him Mari's birth certificate was on its way to him.

"I mailed it to you," Jodi said, telling him he should receive it in three days. "Let me know when you get it."

Jodi disconnected the long distance call and tried to distract herself by imagining seeing her little girl at the airport running into her arms. "Mommy!" Mari would exclaim as she broke free from holding Kevin's hand, running to Jodi's open arms. Jodi imagined kneeling on the floor to be eye-to-eye with her daughter, wrapping her arms around her and feeling the sweet familiar warmth of having her baby back in her arms.

The ride home would be filled with Mari talking non-stop, telling stories of her time in Tehran and describing all of her relatives she got to know. Kevin would smile indulgently, encouraging Mari to keep talking and Jodi would be able to see how tired Kevin really must be after flying halfway around the world with a six-year-old chatterbox.

Days passed, including the day when Kevin should have received Mari's birth certificate. Jodi called again to see if it had arrived.

She was told by Kevin he had not received it yet.

"What can we do if you don't get it in time?" Jodi asked. "Will you still try to come home on the ninth?"

"I might be there, I might not be there," Kevin answered. "I don't have to tell you anything!" he hissed into the phone.

Jodi woke up a couple of days later on July 9 and still hadn't heard whether or not if Mari and Kevin would be flying to the states that day and didn't know what she should do. Were they going to be on the flight, or not? Thoughts shifted in her head recalling Kevin's erratic behavior. But, what if they did make the trip home? What would Kevin do if she wasn't there to meet them?

She decided that she had to go to Dulles. During the drive, Jodi prayed out loud to God.

"Please Father, if it be your will, please let them be there," she prayed with her voice, heart and soul.

Jodi quickly parked her car and practically ran into the airport. "Good," she thought to herself. The plane wasn't scheduled to arrive for another 40 minutes. Always compulsively early, she wanted to be certain that the plane hadn't arrived before she had.

Jodi wasn't certain where they would appear after getting off of the plane. She looked around for something to tell her where to watch for Kevin and Mari.

She saw a man wearing an airport identification tag walk by.

"Excuse me, where will the international passengers be?" Jodi questioned, interrupting him.

"Where are they flying in from?" he asked. She answered that they were traveling from London and he turned to show Jodi where they would be.

"They're coming in from over there," he said pointing across the room.

Chairs lined the wall and Jodi sat down to wait. A monitor flashed the plane's on-time arrival and Jodi anticipated seeing Mari's happy face. An hour passed. Worry danced just outside of her mind, logic telling her that it must be really congested in customs and in the immigration processing lines. She remembered that the airport was constructing an expanded international arrivals building to lessen wait times, but the project wouldn't be finished for another couple of months.

She waited, not willing to give up hope. Two more hours passed. She watched as families were greeted by loved ones, hoping that she would soon be part of a happy reunion of her own. The realization that Mari was not on the flight placed Jodi in a state of frozen. She did not want to allow the thought inside of her mind that she would not see Mari that day. She froze out grief and unbelief. She couldn't give up hope. She dialed Kevin's phone number again. He didn't pick up the call or the several which she made after that.

"I knew that if I got up out of that seat, I would burst into tears," Jodi said. Yet she did manage to go to her car and drive home. Still frozen, tears welled in her eyes making driving difficult but she wouldn't allow herself to cry – not yet.

She redialed Kevin's cell phone repeatedly during the two-hour trip back to Charlottesville. He never answered. What could be happening to them that he wasn't answering? Was Mari safe? Jodi's life became mechanical as she continued to dial.

When she arrived home, to the home that was hers and Mari's, Jodi stood in the kitchen not knowing what to do. What was she feeling; denial, anger or complete helplessness? Her daughter was half-way around the world and she didn't know what was happening.

Jodi sunk down into Mari's favorite living room chair and just stared out of the window. It was Thursday and people had just celebrated the Fourth of July over the weekend while she spent it preparing for the arrival of her precious daughter.

Jodi had purchased a new stuffed bear for Mari and had placed it on her bed, along with new books to read with her at bedtime.

Jodi had received some rest during the past six weeks. Her hair had grown back in and was longer now that the treatments had ended. She had arranged to take a week-long vacation from work which began that day, so she and Mari could just play. She had known she would miss her daughter during the past six weeks, but had never imagined how much.

Jodi knew her mom would be expecting a call from her. She sat staring at nothing for about an hour, feeling frozen. She identified it as bewilderment, not knowing what to do. Mechanically, she dialed her parent's number.

"Hello?" her mother answered. Jodi knew that her mother would listen, no matter what was happening. She knew her mother believed in everything she did and was consistently a voice of encouragement who Jodi knew could feel her pain and hold it as her own.

As Jodi soaked in that hello, she realized she couldn't get any words to come out.

"Jodi, is that you?" her mother asked. Because she was expecting the call, she knew her daughter must be on the other end of the line.

"She wasn't there - they weren't even on the flight . . . I'm not sure what to do," Jodi finally broke down sobbing.

Marilyn's heart broke hearing those words, but as her heart was breaking, she knew Jodi needed her more than ever and ignored her own pain.

"I am so sorry, Sweetie. You will get this straightened out and she'll be home soon," Marilyn soothed. For what seemed like an eternity, mother and daughter shared grief, fear and ideas to get through the coming minutes, hours and days. The two women continued to talk until no more words could be said.

CHAPTER 5

JULY 12, 2009
CHARLOTTESVILLE, VA
(INTERNATIONAL PARENTAL KIDNAPPING)

THREE DAYS LATER KEVIN FINALLY called.

"Why the f*** do you keep calling me? I'm not bringing her home. You've had her for seven years, now I'm keeping her for seven years!" Kevin yelled into the phone, talking as if Mari was a possession and not a child.

Jodi couldn't make sense of what Kevin was saying. This wasn't the Kevin she thought she knew; the laughing and smiling man who adored their daughter and who treated her with kindness. She looked out through the window at his vehicle parked in her driveway and knew that two suitcases filled with his clothing were waiting for him in her guest room.

Nothing was making sense to her. Kevin had hung up abruptly and while Jodi held on to her phone, she just stood in place, staring outside. *What was happening?* She quickly dialed his number again and again and again. No answer.

Around the middle of July, calls from Kevin resumed, but were never predictable. It sounded insane to Jodi to talk to Kevin, who acted as if he were a caring, compassionate father and then another time, talked like a lunatic, asking for money before he would, or could, return Mari.

It was during this time that he repeated he would have her home in time for school. It gave Jodi a little sense of peace because, as erratic as the phone calls had become, a small part of her believed he was really only having money problems, along with difficulties in obtaining a visa, but it would all get worked out.

Jodi had reached out to the State Department to see if it had heard of problems like this in Iran. Specifically, problems to do with required birth certificates, money and such to travel out of Iran. Someone at the State Department told Jodi; because Kevin had said he would have Mari back before school began, to hold on to that hope.

During the next several weeks, Kevin's demeanor continued to be a roller coaster of moods. The week before school was to begin; Kevin's end of their conversations became increasingly violent.

He had started asking Jodi to send money, saying he needed lots of it. He made it very clear that if Jodi wanted to see HIS daughter again, as Mari was his daughter now, Jodi would have to get her hands on a great sum of money and somehow get it to him.

Before Jodi could say anything, he would hang up. Jodi continued to be confused by his actions. Over and over again she would dial Kevin but he wouldn't answer. Jodi wanted to know what he was talking about . . . to know what was *REALLY* going on.

After a time, Jodi got through and he started to repeat the same thing - that Jodi must get him the money if she ever wanted to see Mari again.

Angered and frustrated, Jodi lashed back.

"How much, you bastard! How much do you want in order to bring my daughter back? Two-hundred fifty-thousand dollars? How much?!!!"

"Don't act so dramatic Jodi, this is not a kidnapping. I am her father and I have something you want. Mari. Now you will pay for her!" Kevin demanded before hanging up.

She tried for several days to reach him, but again Kevin refused to answer her calls. Jodi was very upset and so worried about Mari. Did she understand what was happening? Mari had been told she would be home in time for school. Kevin had made that promise to Jodi when he hadn't brought their daughter home on July 9.

Another promise shattered.

She repeatedly checked with the airline to see if Kevin switched tickets, still hoping that he would have Mari back in time to begin first grade. Then, as August went slowly by, it was time for school to begin. Mari had not yet returned home.

The morning of Aug. 25, Jodi drove to Mari's school to see the district superintendent about the situation. She wasn't quite sure what to say yet, but hoped the words would come when necessary. Jodi told them the story that Kevin had told her; he had been detained in Iran because of a passport problem. She knew she couldn't tell them about the erratic phone calls, Kevin's threats and about him asking for money in exchange for Mari. After telling the superintendent the made-up story, Jodi was directed to speak with the elementary school principal and Mari's first grade teacher.

"There's been a problem with Mari's passport," Jodi said, surprised at how calm she could force herself to sound. She was rewarded for her performance with assurances that it would be no problem, that Mari would be welcomed into class as soon as she returned from Tehran.

The following day, Jodi called the State Department and told them Kevin had not returned their daughter for school. She explained the feeling she had from all the erratic phone calls, that he wasn't going to return her and informed the department that he was now asking for money for her safe return.

The State Department representative said they needed Jodi to involve her local authorities to list Mari as missing. She was told that even though she knew where Mari was, she needed a report to open a case of parental abduction. The words hung heavily on Jodi's heart and she couldn't grasp what they were saying.

Parental abduction? What?

The phone conversation ended after they exchanged phone numbers, confirmed Jodi's email address and obtained her promise that she would call local authorities.

Jodi trembled as she dialed the Albemarle County Police to report her daughter as missing.

"Albemarle County Police, how can I help you?"

Jodi summoned all of her strength and courage. "Hi, my name is Jodi Homaune and I need to report my daughter as missing."

As she said the words, tears welled in her eyes so thick she couldn't see. She managed to keep from crying, but she knew her words were mumbled as she told her story.

"Jodi, I am going to send an officer out to meet you. Do you want him to come to your home?"

She knew she wouldn't be able to "keep it together" at home, so she suggested a Starbucks down the road from where she lived.

"That will be fine. He can be there in 30 minutes. Will that be OK?" Jodi was asked.

"Yes, I'll be there," she responded.

Jodi grabbed a folder containing pictures of Mari, her student ID and a copy of her passport.

She arrived early and saw an officer approaching her. He introduced himself and sat down across from Jodi. She felt close to crying.

Who does this? Who calls the authorities and they show up so you can list your child as missing?

Oh my God, what has Kevin done?

"I don't think she's coming home," Jodi tentatively began, after she was asked why she called.

She and Officer Trevor talked for several minutes about Mari and of the circumstances which would lead to listing her as a missing person. Jodi was confused about listing her as "missing," she knew where she was; the problem was that her father refused to bring her home. The Officer explained that listing her as missing was procedure.

When Jodi started to talk about Kevin and the events which had taken place since May 29, the officer said he wanted his partner to hear what she was telling him. He gave him a call and the officer quickly appeared.

Upon meeting his partner, Jodi thought to herself that he looked like a kind, grandfatherly type.

She recited what had taken place over the summer once more and after about 45 minutes of talking, the second officer told Jodi he had a friend in the FBI who was in town.

"I would like you to tell him your story. I think he can help direct us in the right way."

As Jodi sat there with the two officers, they held friendly conversation about Charlottesville and her job at the radio station, which they told Jodi, was their favorite station. Her heart felt like it was pumping out of her chest as she thought about the FBI getting involved. She felt very small sitting next to the two men.

The other people seated outside seemed to be enjoying their gourmet coffees and lunches. Many of them frequently looked over at the trio and Jodi was certain they had become a spectacle. The patrons acted curious as they heard bits and pieces of the conversation and seemed to strain to hear more.

Soon, an FBI Agent approached their table. He appeared to be in his 40s, a slender man dressed in a business suit. Jodi told herself she would not have pegged him as an agent if she had seen him anywhere else. He certainly didn't look like what she imagined an FBI agent would look like.

The FBI Agent squeezed in among the others sitting around the small table and told Jodi to call him John. People who had been there for a while started to watch and stare, not trying to hide their curiosity any longer. John noticed that it made Jodi nervous, and suggested they all move to another location.

Jodi followed the older officer to where the FBI agent was meeting them. She was followed by the police officer with whom she had first met. She drove behind a building she had seen many times at the mall. She wondered where they were taking her as they walked behind some bushes to an unmarked door without a doorknob.

"I would never have guessed what was really behind that door . . ." Jodi marveled.

She entered into a bunker-like office. Bright lights reflected off of its sterile, shiny surfaces. Four other men were there; all looking like police officers. Even though she was treated very kindly, Jodi was fearful. There were now eight of them surrounding her. She recalled she had never felt so odd and safe at the same time. They offered her the use of their restroom and asked her if she wanted tea or coffee.

"It isn't the best, because we're all men here, but it's drinkable," one of the men said, obviously attempting to lighten the mood.

Someone explained to Jodi that Mari needed to be listed as missing, so the procedures to help them could begin. Jodi felt overwhelmed by the reality of the whole situation, after weeks of convincing herself Mari would be home; that Kevin would not keep her in Iran.

"Mrs. Homaune, how old is your daughter?" asked an agent.

For the first time, Jodi began sobbing uncontrollably, allowing herself to truly feel her daughter was being held against her will – and by her own father.

What have you done Kevin? Who are you? He was acting like a stranger.

She recalled the times she had looked at posted pictures of missing and kidnapped children and had wondered how hard it was for their parents to not know what was happening to their children.

"How can these children be missing or lost when the United States is the most powerful nation on earth?" Jodi would silently question. "With all of its resources, why can't they be found?"

She couldn't put herself in their place, imagining the emotions, the real everyday struggles that families and friends of the missing go through. She had no clue what happened inside those families – yet there she was with the FBI to report her only child as missing. The sharp edges of pain began to cut through her frozen exterior.

"I'm not a crier," Jodi began to explain as she tried to speak. "I'm not. The hiccups were now in place as well and Jodi felt she would be perceived as a fool.

"I'm not sure what is happening with Kevin. He doesn't sound like the person Mari and I know," Jodi explained.

She told them of how she felt like she was crawling out of her skin, going mad not knowing what to do.

"I have to help my daughter. Something is wrong and I am not sure how to fix it," she added. (The manic panic she had allowed in did not go away for the next two years.)

The men listened, asking her questions and writing down her answers. She knew that they were in the office for approximately 60 minutes, but it felt longer than that to Jodi.

Once she answered their questions, she was told that Trevor would be the one writing up the report. They told Jodi they agreed with her, that if Mari was listed as missing and Kevin learned that Jodi had involved law enforcement, it would only make things worse.

The FBI agent instructed the officer to make absolutely certain that Mari was not listed on the Internet as missing until the details were sorted out.

The men walked Jodi back to her car. Even though it was only a 30-yard walk, it felt like a mile to Jodi. She felt frozen stiff.

Both officials handed Jodi their cards, in case she had any more questions. She was told she could call anytime day or night and that they would be in touch with her as procedures rolled along. They instructed her to keep trying to talk with Kevin to find out what was happening and to figure out his state of mind.

She got into her Jeep to drive back home and knew her life had shifted. Nothing felt right. She was an optimist, but now doubted her perception of the world.

"I wasn't sure if I should cry because I had listed Mari as missing, or to rejoice knowing I had help. I wasn't alone in this any longer," Jodi said.

Jodi said there are really no words to describe how it feels to be the parent of a missing or kidnapped child.

"It's like walking through Hell," Jodi described in 2012. "The pain it places on your heart is because there is no closure. The unknown keeps you from sleeping, keeps you from functioning normally. It changes who you are and completely changes your surroundings."

She said that most parents have briefly experienced that feeling when their child disappears behind the clothes rack at a department store, or when they turn a corner and cannot see their child for even a second.

"Your heart races and your eyes scan back and forth as manic panic slams into your heart, taking your breath away until you see them again. When you do, you sigh with relief and you smile saying, 'Stay with mommy or daddy and don't do that ever again!'"

CHAPTER 6

October 2009
Charlottesville, VA
(Meeting Robby)

The FBI agent John was very kind to Jodi the first few weeks after Mari was listed as missing. He told her he had children and said he just couldn't imagine what she must be going through. After a short time, he called and told Jodi that her case had been assigned to a new agent and that he wanted to get them together. They agreed to meet at a Dunkin Donuts that was conveniently located halfway between them both.

Her case had been turned over to an agent named Robby, who was assigned to the Richmond Division, Charlottesville Resident Agency.

This is really happening, thought Jodi for the hundredth time. *This is my life without my daughter.*

She arrived at the meeting place ahead of schedule and grabbed a hot tea, so she had something to hold on to as she met her new agent. She didn't know what to expect and sat nervously hoping that the change would be a good thing. What if her case was assigned to an old retired agent, who had exhausted his energy, or worse, his desire to help? With all that was going on in the world with terrorism, she didn't think her missing daughter was going to be a priority with the FBI. There was no "Manual for Dummies" that told parents what to do in the event that their child had been taken away from them.

As John approached her at an outside table, Jodi squeezed her cup and sent a plea heavenward, "Lord, help me through this."

Another man followed the agent and her first impression of Robby took away any doubts she had about his abilities to help. The way he looked at her, directly into her eyes, spoke volumes. He immediately took control of the meeting. He was the first to extend his hand and Jodi shook it, correctly deciding in an instant that he was young enough to possess a lot of energy and to respect the difference in their ages. Just his demeanor instilled a confidence in Jodi that Robby would do everything in his power to get her daughter back and into her arms. Despite his youth, he looked serious and confident and she liked that.

"Please call me Robby, Jodi. I have been looking forward to hearing your story."

After the introductions, John left so she and Robby could get better acquainted. Jodi began by telling Robby everything right up to the moment of their meeting. She wanted him to understand why she thought the situation was ludicrous, so she told him about how she and Kevin met, their marriage, their separation and about their daughter, who was their connection.

Robby took notes and smiled when appropriate. Jodi believed, however, he had no idea about parental abductions at that point. She didn't either. When she was finished with her story, Robby said that the next step was for him to write up a report, look into some things and for Jodi to keep talking to Kevin.

"It may be difficult, but not impossible," Robby concluded about her chances of getting Mari back.

"What do you mean? Our country is the strongest in the world. Mari is just a child. She can't protect herself. I need some help!"

Robby shifted in his chair leaned forward with his elbows resting on his knees. His gaze never left Jodi's face as he explained that their only hope was to get Kevin out of Iran with Mari, because Iran was not a participant in the Hague Abduction Convention Agreement.

"We need to get him to a country where we can help you get her back," Robby explained.

When Jodi returned home, she jumped on to the Internet to learn more about the Hague Convention. She discovered Iran was not one of the 85 countries at the time, listed as participants in the agreement – a treaty enabling the return of a child who had been internationally abducted by a parent, from one member country to another.

Protection under the agreement ensures that a parent who has kidnapped, or who has prevented a child from returning to their rightful home, is prevented from crossing international borders to locate a court which would be sympathetic to the abductor. A child must be younger than 16 to be protected under the convention.

Phone calls between Robby and Jodi remained consistent during the next few months. She reported her contacts with Kevin and Mari to the agent through emails, texts and phone calls. During this time, she was working to gain full custody of Mari and a court had issued Kevin an order for him to return Mari to Albemarle County.

Robby arranged arrest warrants which were in place before the end of the 2010. An Interpol red notice was placed on Kevin for his arrest and extradition and also an Interpol yellow warning on Mari as a person of interest to the United States. It meant that if Kevin or Mari left Iran, authorities would be notified immediately and Kevin would be apprehended and placed in custody and Mari would be kept safe until a U.S. official could reach her. Upon hearing each step as it unfolded, Jodi could not process what was happening, saying it became scarier and scarier to try.

During the final months of 2010 and into early 2011, Jodi had no contact with Kevin or Mari for four months. From November through February, Jodi had no idea how Mari was doing. It was as if they had disappeared altogether.

She continued by making daily phone calls to Kevin's parents, sisters and cousins in Iran. No one answered her calls. She continued her meetings with the State Department, FBI and her lawyers.

She studied about missing children on Internet sites, researched and located lawyers who assisted in international parental abduction.

Then, a package arrived by mail. In the upper left hand corner of the brown paper box was a return address indicating it was from the National Center for Missing and Exploited Children.

"Is that what Mari is now?" wondered Jodi. She knew where Mari was, sort of. She knew at least which part of the world she was in.

Jodi's heart nearly broke as she removed a book from the box. It was an inch and a half thick, bound by a plastic coiled spine. She actually thought she was going to stop breathing. She could hardly take a breath as she processed the words boldly printed on the cover, "Family Abduction – Prevention and Response."

She couldn't even see what was printed inside the book as she turned the pages. Her eyes were filled with pain, tears and disbelief about what was happening. There were 10 tabs in the book, all describing different aspects of parental abduction. There were sections about checklists, civil and criminal remedies and searching for your child.

This was my "Abduction for Dummies" book.

She opened the glossary to read definitions of words she would soon absorb into her everyday language while Mari was gone.

Robby continued to work with Jodi. Plans were made for Mari's rescue to happen in Greece, the Netherlands, Germany, the United States, Canada or Turkey, because the countries had Hague Convention Agreements in place.

Jodi's job was to convince Kevin to allow her to visit Mari and let him know she would bring him money and other things he was requesting. But, first, she had to get him to trust her.

Jodi knew Turkey was a last resort, because she was told that Mari would be placed in Turkey's foster care program as soon as she was there and it could possibly take years in court to get her child out of the country. Jodi would have to literally win back custody of her own daughter.

In discussing with Robby what her options were, Turkey was decidedly their least favorite, making it their last choice.

"We do not want to do Turkey," Jodi firmly decided.

CHAPTER 7

2009
CHARLOTTESVILLE, VA
(FIRST HOLIDAYS WITHOUT MARI)

HALLOWEEN WAS ON A SATURDAY in 2009. Since the year before, Mari had been anticipating Oct. 31 and the fun of dressing up and going door-to-door to trick-or-treat with her friends. In 2008, she had dressed up as a Disney princess – Jasmine. With her long dark hair, big expressive greenish brown eyes against her beautiful olive skin, Jodi thought Mari looked just like the fictional princess featured in Disney's "Aladdin."

Jodi looked out her window at the darkening autumn sky. The trees had dressed up as well in their golds, scarlets and amber colored leaves. She could see candles flickering inside of jack-o-lanterns and knew those were the homes where people would throw open their doors and shriek in surprise when they would see pirates, goblins, princesses and cheerleaders. The entire neighborhood organized the evening so half of her neighbors could go door-to-door, while the other half treated, then the families would switch with the other half, answering doors to hand out candy.

Oh how Mari would enjoy this night.

Where was she? What was she doing? Did she even know it was Halloween? Did she remember how she and her mom would celebrate an entire week beginning with Jodi's birthday on Oct. 27, followed by

Halloween on Oct. 31 and then her own birthday, just a few days later on Nov. 2?

Jodi was not alone that night, thanks to her good friend Liz, who had surprised her with a birthday visit a few days before, unexpectedly showing up on her doorstep.

Liz had called and the two friends were gabbing away like usual.

"What are you planning to do for the next few weeks?" Liz questioned.

Jodi knew that she was really asking how she was going to handle her birthday, Halloween and Mari's birthday that year. She answered that she would basically be in hiding and just trying to get through the coming days. That's what she had been doing plus exercising and trying to figure out what was motivating Kevin to be so possessive of their daughter.

Was he really going to keep Mari?

No! Not again, Jodi thought. She wouldn't allow herself to think like that, taking herself to a place so dark, feeling such extreme loneliness.

"Jodi, JODI! Did you get my package?" Liz asked, shaking Jodi away from her despair. "They were supposed to leave it on your front porch."

She said no and went to look. When Jodi opened her door, Liz was standing right in front of her. The women reached out for each other and began to cry.

"I just can't believe he hasn't brought her back yet," Liz said, holding her friend tight against her.

By 2009, Liz and Jodi had only known each other for a few years, but Jodi knew she was the perfect godmother for Mari. Liz loved the little girl to pieces. Liz was younger than Jodi, and because Mari had been born when Jodi was 38, she felt it was like having two amazing daughters.

"Our age difference spanned many years, but our souls were the same," Jodi described.

A few months before, Liz had traveled with Jodi to get Mari's birth certificate transcribed into Farsi at the Iranian consulate in Washington, D.C. She had learned that an Iranian embassy was not in the United

States, so she was directed to go to the Interests Section of the Islamic Republic of Iran, located at 1250 23rd St. NW.

They entered the building for the first time and had to check in at the bottom of a stairway to state their business.

"I am here to have a birth certificate transcribed into Farsi," Jodi announced. The receptionist directed the women to a door they would find after ascending a few flights of stairs.

As they stepped through the appointed door, a new world was opened up to them. Everything in the room was Persian and very beautiful. From the artwork displayed on the walls to the busts of Iranian leaders, framed maps and upholstered chairs; all of the office décor was elegantly ornate.

Right away Jodi noticed that all of the women were wearing chadors, the gorgeous scarves which cover the head worn mostly by Muslim women. She hadn't thought to bring any for herself or Liz and was worried that she wouldn't be helped because of her oversight.

She took a number and sat down to wait her turn. In time, she heard her number called out and approached the counter. Men were stationed on the other side and appeared to take their jobs very seriously. Jodi was relieved to hear they spoke fluent English and so she told them why she was there.

"Why is your child in Iran? Why did you let her go in?" they questioned her.

She told them that they were visiting Kevin's family and that he said he needed the document to get Mari an Iranian passport, so she could travel out of the country. The men took the document Jodi had and stared at her for a very long time, most likely to determine if she was telling the truth.

The man who was helping her had a kind look on his face when he told Jodi that Kevin didn't need Mari's birth certificate for that purpose. He explained that Mari could use her father's passport, which was law in Iran.

"I'm not sure what to do, but I do need her birth certificate transcribed, her father is demanding it and he is saying it will get her home." Jodi replied softly.

Is Kevin telling the truth? I have to believe he is.

She was told to wait and stood at the counter while the man went into another office.

When he returned, he said that they would have the birth certificate transcribed, but that she would have to return in one week. In the meantime, they would be checking Kevin's information filed in Iran.

"We will do this for you because you are the mother and she belongs back in the United States," the man told Jodi, before turning away.

As she and Liz left the building, she felt so much better knowing that the Iranian representatives were going to help her. She called Kevin to tell him that the document would be delayed one week.

"Thank you," Kevin said.

Obviously in a kind mood, Kevin allowed Jodi to speak with Mari. For about three minutes they spoke about the weather and that Jodi was getting paperwork done so that Mari could come home. Mother and daughter exchanged, "I love you's," and blew kisses across the miles. The next thing she heard was Kevin's voice.

"Get this job done Jojo, or you won't see Mari again!"

All the good feelings drained out of Jodi as Liz watched her expression go from happy and elated to dark and despairing.

A week passed and Liz and Jodi traveled again to D.C., this time bringing chadors with them, out of respect for the Iranian culture. They had practiced putting them on before they left Jodi's home. When they arrived at the Interests Section, the women secured the chadors over their heads and Jodi looked at her friend. She became teary thinking what a great friend Liz was to walk with her through this part of her journey.

Liz had never questioned wearing the chador, or anything she was doing with Jodi, just standing with her and doing what had to be done for Mari. Liz was a natural beauty, inside and out and looked truly amazing wearing her head covering. She was tall with dark brown hair and gorgeous blue eyes. Jodi said that when Liz walked into a room, everyone noticed her. Not only was she physically beautiful, she was smart and very kind.

They signed in and climbed the stairs. Several Iranians passed the American women and just looked at them. As Jodi had learned, the Iranian culture is a warm, very friendly culture. Its people are outgoing and strangers are treated like people they haven't had the opportunity to get to know.

When Jodi's number was called, she approached the counter at the window and was face-to-face with the same older Iranian man who assisted her the week before. He smiled at her.

"I knew I had his approval and was smart to cover my head," said Jodi.

He took the paper Jodi handed to him, telling her it would take some time to have it translated and transcribed. The certificate would then be stamped with the Islamic Republic of Iran seal, making it legally recognized in Iran.

Jodi and Liz watched people come and go for hours and were the only Americans in the room during the whole time. No one spoke to them, yet would nod in greeting as they walked past. Jodi sensed that they were questioning why she had to be there. Jodi and Liz continued to talk softly between themselves and continued to wait.

Finally after four hours, Jodi was summoned to the counter and was handed the transcribed certificate bearing an official seal. The process had cost $50 and Jodi felt like she was one step closer to seeing her daughter.

"Good luck. Your daughter needs to be back on U.S. soil," she was told again, before she left.

Back in Charlottesville, Jodi just couldn't fathom entertaining trick or treaters on Halloween with the dark thoughts crowding her mind, wondering what was happening to Mari. She checked again to make sure her porch light was off and sat down with Liz. The women spent all night talking, strategizing how to get Mari back. Mari was missing out on so much.

Two days later it was Mari's seventh birthday. Jodi had sent gifts to her in Tehran – a Pez dispenser, coloring books, new crayons, a stuffed dog and a new winter jacket. She wondered if her daughter received them in time and if Kevin and his family were celebrating the event with the precious seven-year-old. She tried to imagine the look on Mari's face when she opened her gifts, tearing the paper off and throwing it to the side, digging to get to treasures unknown.

Family and friends called to chat with Jodi, but she knew that they were only trying to take her mind off of Mari's absence. She tried calling Kevin for an opportunity to talk to Mari, but didn't get an answer. She soon learned that she was only "allowed" to speak with Mari, not on the day of a special occasion, but only days after a major American holiday or birthday. Then, Jodi would have to listen to Kevin say that Mari had the "best" holiday or birthday ever while she was away from her mother.

Christmases in the Homaune Virginia home, for the most part, were quiet with Mother and daughter celebrating their favorite time of year and enjoying the holiday season. Ever the one for traditions, Jodi always prepared a birthday cake to welcome Baby Jesus and did so in 2009, without Mari. Christmas Day especially was always peaceful. Mari would open her presents from Santa Clause and the day would be filled with phone calls to family and Mari giggling the whole day long.

On Jodi's first Christmas Eve without Mari, she burned a candle all night long into Christmas morning. She had read about a custom which states if a candle burns brightly through the night, a wish she wished would come true.

Gathering all the candles she could find, she melted them all together and made a large candle. As the sky darkened, Jodi touched a match to the candle's wick and its flame was bright and beautiful. Jodi watched it long before sleep claimed her.

She suddenly awoke at six o'clock the next morning. She looked at the candle and witnessed it flicker once before it extinguished itself. Jodi was sure that God wanted her to know the candle stayed illuminated all night and that her wish was going to come true.

CHAPTER 8

2010
CHARLOTTESVILLE, VA
(A VERY, VERY LONG YEAR)

JODI WAS NOT ALLOWED TO talk to Mari for four months, from November through March 2010. She thought it may have been because of a welfare check she asked for from the Swiss Embassy in Tehran. In late January 2010, Jodi had not spoken to Mari since after her birthday in early November and once two months of no contact had passed, the State Department recommended to Jodi that she initiate a welfare check on her daughter.

Jodi was told that there was no U.S. embassy in Iran, because of what had happened with a hostage event in the 1980s. So, the Swiss Embassy worked with the United States regarding the welfare of American citizens who were in Iran. In concert with the State Department, it agreed that they would perform a welfare check. In September 2009, Jodi had filled out welfare check documents in the event she wanted to use them, never dreaming she would have to.

She learned an embassy representative would go to the place where Mari was staying and leave notice for Kevin that the Swiss Embassy wanted to see both of them. If he and Mari did not show up for the appointment, then Kevin would warrant further investigation.

A notice was sent informing Kevin that he was expected to come to the embassy on Tuesday, March 2. According to a report from the

State Department, Kevin had phoned the embassy that morning to postpone the visit until the next day, "on the pretext that since Mari's school was out on Wednesday, it was more convenient for him to drop by on Wednesday," per the document shared with Jodi.

Jodi received the completed report, with photos of her daughter on March 11, eight days following the welfare check.

Tears rolled down her face as she looked at photographs of her daughter. It had been 10 months since she had seen Mari and she could hardly bear the pain as she remembered her so full of life and happy the last time she saw her, now looking so sad ...and different. Her hair had been chopped off and she was sitting with her hands clasped together. She looked scared and dejected.

"It was truly like her life had been stolen and she was a little girl just existing," Jodi recalled. That's when her attitude took a 180 degree swing. She went from thinking, *"Kevin, what have you done?"* to *"What have I done?"* She had trusted that man and always believed he had loved his daughter more than himself. He had proved that. Or had he really?

Jodi then began believing that what happened to Mari must be her own fault, for believing in Kevin for more than seven years. She wondered how she could have been so blind.

The report didn't say much that meant anything to the FBI or Jodi, but seeing the photos gave her the strength she was praying for, to continue. She knew then that Mari needed her more than she ever could have imagined.

The report revealed that Mari appeared to be in good health and spirits and acted a little shy during her meeting at the embassy. Mari told the investigator that she was in first grade and had five friends. Her father reported that he and his family were taking very good care of Mari and took her to and from school every day. Her grandmother stayed with her after school. On the weekends, the family would take Mari to the mountains, on picnics and other excursions. He said that they provided her with clothes and that she did not have to cover her hair. Kevin also pointed out that he encouraged Mari to keep up with her English and showed her children's movies, which were in English, to prove his point.

"Mari is very happy here," according to a quote by Kevin.

After the welfare check, Kevin called Jodi and was explosive, questioning Jodi as to who did she think she was questioning his parenting abilities.

Jodi quickly told him that because Mari was an American citizen, that the welfare check was done on behalf of the United States government and that neither she nor he had a choice in the matter. She heard him calm down and so she asked to speak with Mari.

"No. You will not talk to her Jodi, until we straighten a few things out," Kevin answered and hung up.

At least she had spoken to Kevin, counting it as a contact. The past months of not hearing anything was the worst Jodi had known. The feelings she experienced were of total helplessness, and with her connection to Mari severed, there was nothing she could do until Kevin answered her phone calls or he made contact. So, she kept studying, contacting anyone she could think of, and continued to work with Robby.

Jodi was granted full legal custody of Mari on June 2; however, she didn't recognize her life anymore. At the time of Mari's kidnapping, Jodi was working as a sales manager for six radio stations, supervising nine to 12 salespeople. When Mari was not returned in the summer of 2009, Jodi asked to be relieved of her supervisory duties and demoted to salesperson, so that her schedule was more flexible. She needed more time to work with the authorities in trying to get her daughter back.

After six weeks selling for a radio station, Jodi was fired from her job and performed bathroom renovations for a friend. In 2010 and into 2011, Jodi accepted commission-only sales jobs when she could, with several different employers. She went from earning nearly $82,000 in 2008 to $14,000 in 2011. She did so to be able to leave the country at a moment's notice, in the event Kevin would agree to a visit, or to let her bring Mari home.

Kevin began to talk to Jodi in October about visiting Mari. He said he was ready to return to the United States and to Canada. Jodi quickly arranged for airline tickets to be purchased where Kevin could pick them up via the Internet and fly out of Iran in December. Kevin and Mari would fly from Tehran to Amsterdam and then on to Dulles. He indicated that he had moved from Tehran to another city called Mashhad, but they would fly out of Tehran.

"I will need money Jodi," Kevin said at the time. He said he needed reassurance from her that she had money available for him to use, plus a car and personal items; namely a computer and credit cards in his name.

"Is my permanent resident card still good?" he asked. "If you want to see my daughter, you have to convince me that you have not charged me with her kidnapping," Kevin demanded.

Because Jodi had been Kevin's sponsor for his permanent residency card, all of his debts had to be assumed by her. Thousands and thousands of dollars in credit card debt had been racked up by Kevin before he left. Prior to the trip to Iran, Kevin had never left a balance on his cards, Jodi recalled. Having no choice, she started paying on some of the card balances and calling the creditors, but they would not provide her with any account information. She thought maybe that they were being held as evidence.

Conversations continued between Kevin and Jodi during November of 2010, with Jodi having no phone contact with Mari. Communication with her daughter had become extremely limited once again and Jodi knew Kevin would not let her speak with Mari on her birthday or later that month on Thanksgiving.

The list of what Jodi could not say to Mari, as dictated by Kevin, continued to grow.

"I wasn't allowed to tell her about anything in America. I couldn't mention her grandparents, uncles, aunts, cousins, or her friends from school. I was only allowed to tell her that I loved her - but I could not talk about her coming home and I could not tell her how much I missed her," Jodi said.

Jodi dialed Kevin's phone number on Dec. 11.

"What do you want?" he answered.

Jodi could instantly tell he was agitated. She was becoming familiar with his changing moods but never could predict which Kevin would answer – the kind man she knew from before or the one who was becoming more familiar; angry and agitated. She braced herself to speak with the latter.

"There is no reason for the December visit – we are not coming!" Kevin started screaming at Jodi. "Listen, I have made Mari's memory of you bad. How else do you think I convinced her to stay! I have told her that if we came back to the states you would never let me see her. I have told her that you are nothing but a whore and you always had strange men around her and I brought her to Iran to protect her from you and all your men."

He told her that he knew what he was saying was not true, but that Mari did not.

"So, there is no reason for you to ever talk to Mari again. She thinks you are trash and is afraid of you. Go f*** yourself and go f*** the United States!" The call disconnected and Jodi knew they weren't voluntarily coming back home.

Kevin told Jodi during that conversation that she should have known he was an Iranian and that everything he told her when they were together was all lies. She was instructed to go to the Internet and look up Iranian men and read about them. Then, Jodi would know what kind of life Mari was going to have.

The conversation had Jodi thinking that Kevin had lost his mind. She knew other Iranian men, and wondered why he was trying to scare her. Why was he continuing to flip his stories about coming and not coming? He was acting insane.

The next day, Jodi called Kevin and he answered the phone again, sounding much calmer. He explained that the U.S. trip was off and that he would not come and meet her because he learned that she had filed a complaint against him.

"I don't know who to believe," Kevin admitted.

Jodi was learning to play his game and began to try and build his confidence. She didn't care what the FBI did with him once they returned. She just wanted to make sure Mari was safe and loved.

"Just come back home," Jodi said, feigning concern. She assured him that no charges had been made against him and that he was not in any kind of trouble. After all, she was the sponsor of his permanent residency card and they shared a daughter.

Kevin continued to tell her if she wanted to talk with Mari, she would have to pay. Send money to talk with Mari, was Kevin's mantra. He laughed as he said, "You're not stupid Jodi, send the money."

Jodi told Kevin she had a plan. Kevin could stay with her and Mari in Virginia. She said she had enough money which he could use to get back on his feet. Jodi said she could get him the credit cards he wanted, that all of his previous debts had been paid and that his precious BMW was sitting in the garage, waiting for him.

Kevin tentatively agreed, telling Jodi it would only happen if she would meet him at a location where an Iranian embassy was located for his protection and they could fly back to the United States together.

Come on out Kevin.

CHAPTER 9

2011
CHARLOTTESVILLE, VA
(DEMANDS)

KEVIN DID NOT ANSWER THE phone again until late January 2011. He discussed meeting Jodi in March, because Mari would be out of school for two weeks.

He requested Jodi bring to him $10,000 in cash, a laptop computer and walkie talkies, as part of their agreement to meet. Kevin said he would give her specific details on which brands to buy, as the meeting got closer. He made it very clear to her that he would only allow Mari to visit with her, plus, if she brought what he asked for, he would consider permitting Mari to go back home with Jodi.

Jodi said that Kevin was sounding kind and soft spoken during the calls; acting like he was the victim in the mess he had created.

He described Mari as thriving, loving school and loving her life in Iran.

"She sure misses you Jojo, but not enough to say she wants to go home, cause if she did, I would bring her there," Kevin said boastfully.

At that point, Jodi knew he was purposely trying to hurt her. It was too late for that, she thought. He hadn't yet figured out that she had learned very early on to be careful with every single word she spoke to him. It was imperative that she controlled every word, every emotion.

In order for Jodi to "visit" Mari, she had to agree that it would be on Kevin's terms and in a country of his choosing. He said he was not going to be placed in a situation where she tricked him, so that her f****** government could interfere with him, or disrupt his life. He kept repeating his terms, which created even more worries about Mari's wellbeing; something Jodi hadn't thought could be possible.

Kevin now wanted to meet Jodi in the Middle East, in Dubai. Jodi was advised by Robby that she should not meet him there.

"We can't help you in Dubai, Jodi," Robby told her. "It's not safe for you to travel alone and we can't guarantee that you and Mari could get out safely."

She knew she had to convince Kevin that she wasn't allowed into the country with her chemo medicines because customs would not allow it and so they had to find another place.

It worked, because Kevin had believed that Jodi was receiving chemo treatment for her throat. In an earlier conversation, Kevin had asked Jodi about her neck surgery, which opened a door to talk about new medicines she could say were preventing her to travel to certain places.

Jodi began focusing on trying to convince Kevin to meet her in Greece, because she was told Greek authorities were aware of her situation and had agreed to help her if she could talk Kevin into traveling to Athens.

Jodi said Robby was never able to tell her exactly what to say to Kevin. He instructed her to stay calm and always to try to keep him calm.

"I started telling Kevin that I would pay for everything if he could just meet me in Athens – tickets, money, hotel and food. I would bring anything he wanted, if I could just get to see Mari." Jodi said that she was very careful about using the word "visit," and to never say, "to bring Mari home."

After 17 months of despairing, Jodi began hoping.

Then, Kevin suggested something she never had imagined. He declared that he would not be bringing Mari with him to Greece to meet

Jodi. If Jodi behaved during their meeting and was a "good person," he would "allow" her to see her daughter at some future date.

Jodi seriously thought she had just conversed with the Devil himself. Kevin had just told her that there was no need for Jodi to see Mari at that time or probably anytime.

"She doesn't need a mother anymore. She has forgotten all about you. I have made sure she thinks bad of you and your country," said Kevin, sounding eerily calm.

Mari doesn't deserve this, thought Jodi, her anger increasing at what he was doing. Her resolve to sound calm became stronger as her heart continued to break again and again. Jodi leaned on God in prayer to give her the strength to continue her charade.

Why did Kevin want to meet with Jodi alone? She knew Kevin recognized how desperate she was to see Mari; he must believe that she would do anything he asked of her.

"He was right. I was desperate, but not stupid enough to believe he wasn't going to get rid of me after he got his money and the other things he wanted," Jodi determined.

For weeks, Jodi tried to call Kevin. Neither he nor his family would answer her calls. Once again, Jodi felt helpless. The roller coaster of dealing with Kevin began to take its toll and Jodi knew she couldn't allow herself to let it go, because she had to help Mari.

Then in April, on a Friday afternoon, when the trees were greening and flowers were springing up, Jodi heard her sweet daughter's voice.

"Hi Mommy!"

Jodi could hardly believe it was Mari. When she saw the number on caller ID, she assumed it was Kevin finally getting in touch again.

"Hello, Mari?"

The telephone connection was clear. Cautiously Jodi said, "I love you Sweetie, how are you?"

Surprisingly, Mari wasn't pulled from the phone. Jodi's thoughts were spinning with delight, yet she was cautious in trying to figure out what was really happening. Mari had never called from Iran by herself and Jodi wondered if Kevin was playing another game.

"OK," Mari responded meekly, sounding scared and rushed. She was almost whispering.

"I am not supposed to be on the phone with you when my Baba is not here."

Jodi quickly asked her if she was at her grandmother's house.

"Yes, I am at Grandma Batool's."

Jodi instinctively knew then that Mari was telling the truth. Her father really wasn't there.

"Mari, listen to me," Jodi instructed. "I want you to know that I love you very much and I am doing everything I can to get you back home. We will be together again. Please believe it in your heart. Keep remembering how much Mommy loves you, no matter what you are told," Jodi said, feeling like she was racing against time to get all the words out.

"I know, Mama," said Mari, before the phone went dead.

"Mari, are you still there?" Jodi said over and over. "Mari? Mari!"

What was happening? Who dialed the phone for her? Was she really alone at her grandmother's?

Jodi repeatedly dialed Kevin's parent's house, with no one picking up. She decided against calling Kevin, sensing that perhaps Grandma Batool had dialed the phone and was trying to help Mari.

Jodi did not know if Kevin's mother was aware of his behavior. Even if she had known Kevin was acting so erratically, there was nothing she would do. She would not be able to stand against her son in Iran. It wasn't in their culture for her to tell him it was time to send Mari home. From what she knew about her, Jodi believed that if Kevin's mother knew what he was doing, that she might even think it was wrong, but would never voice her opinion.

Mari's voice had been so soft when she spoke, yet she sounded so happy to be speaking with her mother. It had all happened so fast, so Jodi went into her state of being frozen to recall hearing Mari's voice over and over in her head. She hoped and prayed that Mari could understand what she had told her because Jodi knew she was speaking in a rush. She offered a prayer to God to keep Mari safe. She prayed that her daughter's little heart understood that Jodi would find her and bring her home.

She counted the call as a sweet blessing.

"I believe that God knew that both Mari and I needed that phone call at that time," Jodi said.

She contacted Robby to report Mari's call and to let him know she needed to step-up her game in getting Kevin to travel out of Iran. She stayed awake for the following 48 hours that weekend, doing push-ups, sit-ups, studying Farsi and researching places where she and Kevin could meet.

"I was feeling lonely, but felt powerful that I could complete my mission to bring Mari home," Jodi recalled.

She knew that it would be a struggle and that she would have to be in the best shape, both physically and emotionally, to accomplish the mission.

At this point in Jodi's journey, Mari had been gone for nearly two years. Jodi had isolated herself and continued living in her black and white world.

"Every second of every day, I thought about ways to get Mari home," Jodi said. What I did wasn't healthy, and I wouldn't recommend it, but it is what I had to do."

Later that month, Kevin called and again began talking about meeting Jodi. She could tell by the tone of his voice that he didn't know Mari had called her. Jodi secretly smiled about how brave Mari had been to make the call, but prayed she stayed safe and that her father would never find out that Mari had called her.

After Mari was home, Jodi finally learned about the phone call made in April 2011. Mari said her dad had gone away for two days and had left her in her grandmother's care. Before he left, Kevin had left specific instructions with his mother that Mari was not to go outside or to tell anyone she was American and absolutely was not allowed to talk to Jodi if she called. They were not to answer any long distance phone calls at all.

After her father left, Mari begged her grandmother to let her call her mother. She was crying and upset about not being able to go back home. Her grandmother relented and said she would dial Jodi's number and that Mari could talk to her mother for a few seconds, "very few," she emphasized. Mari was also told that she could never tell her father about the call or they would be punished and beaten.

Mari continued telling her Mother that Grandma Batool knew she should be back in the United States with her mother and that she believed her mom to be a good person. Mari said she promised never to tell and so, her grandmother dialed the phone for her.

After talking with her mother, Mari said that her grandmother hugged her and told her she knew her mother would find a way to be with her again. Mari said it made her feel good to hear Jodi's voice and what she had said. It made her know that Jodi would find her and that she would be out of the situation she was in with her father.

"I hated him so much at this point because of the beatings and the lies. I felt terrible and believed it was my fault. I wanted just to go home and be with you, Mom," Mari later confided.

Kevin said he wanted her to send him money through the mail, even though Jodi had explained to him over and over again that it was illegal to send U.S. currency that way. Kevin became irate and told Jodi if she loved their daughter, she would find a way to send it. He suggested she go to the Washington, D.C. travel agency he used to purchase his air travel to Iran to ask if they knew how to get money to him in Iran. He reminded Jodi of what he had told her before, that Iranians have a way of getting money to each other by giving someone money which is transferred through a network of people until it ends up in Iran.

Kevin requested that Jodi call him in a few weeks to talk about meeting together and said he wanted to hear that she had visited the travel agency to ask them about getting money to him.

Jodi called the agency to find out if the woman named on the airline tickets Kevin used still worked there. She hoped not, so she could use that as a reason why she couldn't send the money. She knew that sending the money wouldn't matter, it wouldn't bring Mari back.

"I knew deep in my heart, the money was not going to Mari and to help them get out of Iran," said Jodi.

She thought that Kevin was using money as ransom, so that Jodi could see Mari. Jodi looked up the meaning of ransom and couldn't believe Kevin had resorted to using the tactic. He, of course, would never say it was a kidnapping or parental abduction for money, but it became obvious that was exactly what he was doing.

> Ransom   *noun;*-1. the redemption of a prisoner, slave, or kidnapped person, of captured goods, etc., for a price.
> *verb*; 1. to redeem from captivity, bondage, detention, etc., by paying a demanded price.

The stars were in order as she called the travel agency. She was told that the Iranian woman from whom Kevin had purchased the tickets, no longer worked there. Jodi told Kevin they would not talk with her because she was not Iranian, hoping that Kevin would realize that particular delivery avenue was closed to her. At that point, he was demanding $25,000.

Osama Bin Laden was killed by U.S. military forces on May 2, 2011 and the news was broadcast all over the world. Because of Kevin's bizarre behavior, Jodi worried about how the news would affect her efforts in gaining Kevin's trust to bring him out of Iran with Mari. She had talked with Robby about what she had found out at the travel agency. During their conversation, he said he understood her concerns about how Kevin would react to the news of Bin Laden's death.

CHAPTER 10

May 10, 2011
Charlottesville, VA
(Mother's Day weekend)

Jodi woke up on Mother's Day with a hopeful heart that she would be able to talk with Mari.

"After she was born, every day was Mother's Day for me," Jodi said.

She sometimes thought her perspective on motherhood was because she was older than the average mom when she gave birth to Mari, and also knowing that Mari would be her only child.

"I loved being her mom!" She also loved being a unique family of two. Kevin was a part of their lives, a major part, but family to Jodi meant herself and Mari, a family consisting of a single mother raising her only child, her daughter.

The morning air was warm and so Jodi had gone outside to sit on her porch. At the time, she was renting a room from a family in Charlottesville and they had gone away for the weekend. As she sat on a chair with a cup of tea in the mellow morning light, she dialed Kevin's number, allowing herself to get excited as she anticipated hearing Mari's voice. Since her last conversation with her daughter, her voice had never left Jodi's mind. The sweet memory haunted her.

"Don't ever call here again you mother f****** American," Kevin answered in the scariest voice Jodi had ever heard come out of him. He was screaming at the top of his lungs. Jodi was instantly rocked to the core, which caused her heart to race. She quickly tried to think about how to diffuse the situation.

"What is wrong? Why are you screaming?" She tried to sound calm but firm and in control. Her throat was tight with tension and she hoped her hoarseness didn't betray her emotions. She might as well have saved her voice because Kevin continued as if he hadn't heard her questions.

"Why don't you send in your American Army to capture Mari like you did Osama! In fact why don't you go f*** the generals and see if they will help you? Do you think they give a s*** about Mari or you? You think, like them, that you can do anything you want because you are American!"

On hearing Kevin's accusations, Jodi's defenses wrapped around her and she became frozen again because she knew that she couldn't do anything to calm him. Out of habit, she plugged in a recorder to document the conversation and took notes in case the recorder didn't work. Her hands were shaking so much that her writing looked like chicken scratch. Her chest hurt so badly that Jodi honestly thought that Kevin's rants might be causing her to have a heart attack! She couldn't figure out what to do; she couldn't even make sense of what he was saying.

"I want you to know something Jojo. I will kill Mari before I send her back to that mother f**** country! Do you hear me? I will kill Mari before she ever sees you again and if I can't make it in Iran, I will end our lives," screamed Kevin, sounding like a psychopath. He continued.

"If she lives to be 18 and wants to see you, I will kill her before I will let that happen!" Before Jodi could answer, she heard a click and then silence. Kevin had disconnected the call.

Jodi was shocked once again. She thought she had heard the absolute maximum of his madness, but this was beyond anything he had said before. She believed he would actually kill his daughter before letting her come home. It was the second time Kevin had threatened to harm Mari in two years. She had never before thought Kevin was even capable of thinking that he could.

Jodi's thoughts quickly went back in time to the day in court when she gained full custody of Mari. She testified that Kevin was threatening to sell his daughter on the black market if she didn't meet his demands. She had taken the threat very seriously at that time but many months had passed since the threats. Kevin had started to work on their meeting and Jodi had pushed the threat to the back of her mind.

Because Jodi had been on the receiving end of so much violent verbal abuse about the person she loved most in the world, she was really confused. Her thought process wasn't logical any longer. Her first thought was that she had to call her mother and wish her a happy Mother's Day. Then, she thought about how throughout the United States, families were wishing their loved ones the same; going to church and out to eat or gathering for family dinners in freshly mowed back yards. It made her feel at peace for a few seconds.

Then her thoughts came rushing back and it sunk in – someone she had once trusted had just threatened to kill her daughter.

Jodi's face was wet with tears which flowed at a pace she had never shed before. Nothing she had been through had hurt so much. She struggled with thoughts to fight back, remembering his threats; trying to keep her terror at bay and only concentrate on how to get Mari home and out of his hands.

By then, she had curled herself up into a ball on the patio. Eventually she passed out, apparently from being so upset. An hour passed before she awoke on the porch, still clutching the phone in her hand. She knew she couldn't give in to the pains in her chest and head. She had to get Mari home.

After time had passed, she felt she was back in control over her body and emotions. She called Robby to tell him what had just happened. When he answered, Jodi began saying she had contacted Kevin, but before she could complete the sentence, she broke down again.

Robby was a rock, sensing something horrible had just occurred. There had been times in the past two years when she had cried in front of Robby and Donna; when tears flowed for brief moments and they viewed Jodi wiping her eyes. This break down was much worse than any that Robby had witnessed. The fact that it was Mother's Day made it even more heart wrenching.

Robby kept prompting Jodi, telling her to take her time as she told him what happened. It took Jodi about an hour to tell him the story, which normally would have taken just 20 minutes. While sitting in the strengthening sunlight, she rehashed the one-sided conversation with Kevin. She felt a renewed connection with humanity as Robby said he also was taking Kevin's threats very seriously.

"Robby always made me feel better after every conversation. He was always patient and understanding, telling me to take my time and that I had done a great job when talking with Kevin," said Jodi.

"Keep up the good work Jodi, you're doing super," he would say.

She often chuckled to herself after talking with Robby and hearing his encouragement. She knew he meant well; however, she did not think she was ever doing enough.

"I always thought that I needed to do more."

Later that night, after she had "pulled together" Jodi called her mother.

When she heard her mother's voice, Jodi became emotional once again, causing her mother to cry as well. There are certain words which cannot be easily processed, such as a parent threatening to kill their child. It is impossible for something like that to resonate in the brain. There is no logic to it and acknowledging it forces panic up to the surface. Jodi managed to finish her conversation with her mother by saying that she was fine and would call her again the next day.

She knew her mom had been shaken by the most recent threat from Kevin and that she would share the news with her dad who hadn't been feeling well the past few weeks. Appointments had been scheduled with his cardiologist, so Jodi knew her mother would convey Jodi's news to her father carefully and with gentleness, possibly not telling him everything.

In the first few months after Mari was gone, Jodi's dad had called and asked her to send him a current photo of his granddaughter. He said he wanted to carry it in his wallet, so he would have it close to look at. He said it would bring good luck to do so and would help in getting Mari back home.

To this day, Jodi says that her father has never taken the photo out of his wallet. Whenever his wallet is opened, the first thing which can be seen is a photo of Mari when she was six. Mari was Jodi's father's only granddaughter and his youngest grandchild.

"They have a special bond full of fun, laughter and love. My dad fell in love with Mari the first time he held her when she only weighed 3 pounds. That image of him holding her kept me feeling strong and determined, even when I thought there was no hope," Jodi said.

Jodi tried calling Kevin for weeks. She would dial his number six times during a 24-hour period. She would try every four hours, a routine which worked to keep her feeling sane.

"I would dial Kevin's number . . . no answer. I would then try different family members whose numbers I had . . . no answer. I would set an alarm to wake me during the night so I could make more calls," Jodi described. She said that the time difference between the U.S. and Iran made the schedule easy to keep.

During the hours between the call attempts, she studied Farsi. She also aggressively exercised, doing anything to keep her mind occupied and doing something useful to help get Mari home.

During the first week of June, she was shocked to hear Kevin finally answer his phone with a voice she recognized from before his perfidy, his betrayal. He sounded like the man she had once loved. He acted like his last call to her the month before had never happened.

"Jojo, I want to talk about meeting," he said calmly. "I want you to see Mari and she needs to see you."

Jodi knew better than to discuss the possibility of bringing Mari home with her.

"I needed to keep building his trust so he would bring her with him out of Iran. I could sense he was going to let me talk with Mari and the thought thrilled me," Jodi said.

Kevin said that he had told Mari that she may be visiting her mother soon.

"Make no mistakes Jojo, you will bring some things I need and if you do this, I will allow you to visit Mari but she will not be going home with you." The last was said distinctly, evidently so Jodi would not misunderstand him.

Even though his voice was level and soft, Jodi could hear the steel resolve just beneath the surface.

Jodi, herself was playing the same game and forced herself to sound calm. In the weeks following his last phone call, her focus on her mental and physical health had resulted in her becoming stronger. She was ready for him.

"I knew I was going to bring Mari home. Either he was going to bring her out, or I was planning to go into Iran and bring her out myself," said Jodi.

While she was directing sales at the radio stations, Jodi had met some really amazing people in Charlottesville working charity functions with the American Red Cross, the National Kidney Foundation and the American Cancer Society. After her daughter was abducted, Jodi had reached out to an acquaintance, which was well-connected in an organization involved in charity work around the world.

Jodi was told that the organization could help her after she described her circumstances. Particularly, if she couldn't convince Kevin to travel with Mari, Jodi was putting a plan together to go to Iran to check on Mari. At that time, she did not think she would be able to take her daughter out of the country, but would be able to see for herself if she was OK. She had read the book, *Not Without My Daughter* many times over and had watched the Sally Field movie version of the book and was now living the story.

There were differences such as Betty Mahmoody was trying to get out of Iran with her daughter and Jodi was trying to get in to Iran to get her daughter.

She was careful not to tell Robby or Donna what she was planning. She knew they would not have recommended it. It was not safe or intelligent but Jodi didn't worry about that. She had purchased brown contacts to cover her blue eyes and knew that by bleaching her brown hair blonde, no one would recognize her and probably think she was one of many charitable volunteers. It would work. It had to.

Jodi did not know exactly where Mari was living in Iran, but had addresses of Kevin's family. She had begun studying where their homes were located and she continued to study Farsi. Her studies were crucial to her plans. Her parents, siblings and other family would be left behind, yet she couldn't care.

"I had no life without Mari and my motherly instincts were telling me to either lure him out of Iran, or for me to go to Mari.

Their phone conversation continued. Kevin said he wanted to meet in Baku, Azerbaijan. She knew that Robby would say that wouldn't be possible, but told Kevin she would check to see if she could obtain a visa to travel to the country. Azerbaijan was a country with no direct ties with the United States and would not assist in their efforts to bring Mari home.

"Please, can I talk to Mari?" Jodi asked Kevin, since he seemed agreeable. "It has been a long time since I have had the chance to tell her I love her."

Kevin paused and then said she could, only if she would not talk to Mari about returning home.

"She believes if you act like a good person, she will be able to visit you."

Jodi assured him that all she wanted to do was to tell to Mari how much she loved her.

"Hello?" Once again her daughter sounded so small and wilted.

"Hi Mari!"

"Hi Mommy."

"I love you Mari!"

"I love you too Mommy."

Jodi strained to hear any semblance of her child. Mari sounded so meek, certainly not the fun loving giggling girl she was before. She heard the phone being taken away and Kevin telling Jodi to check out Baku and to make it work.

"Call me in three days," Kevin said gruffly, before hanging up.

As delighted as Jodi was to hear Mari's voice, she could hear echoes of pain in the few words Mari spoke to her. If Kevin was treating Mari the way he was treating her, how was Mari really doing? Was she being brainwashed to think that her mother was a bad person? That would explain her meekness. Was she sad and missing her mother? Did she even remember Jodi? Jodi just didn't know the answer to those questions and it was driving her mad.

During the first few months after the abduction, the thoughts would make Jodi feel sad, pushing her back into a state of darkness. Questions having no answers and thoughts whirled around in her head with no place to settle. Now, thanks to God, Jodi was fortified with a special "Mommy Power," an inner strength; not her own. It felt like she was playing a part in a movie.

"My will to get Mari home was all I thought about and the motivation behind everything I did," Jodi said.

No longer in a puddle of tears after talking with Kevin, or vomiting as she usually did after one of his calls, Jodi could feel herself becoming a power house. She felt like she could control her actions and do what she had to do. She met with the State Department, the FBI and friends. No one was aware of what she was thinking or planning if Kevin couldn't be lured out of Iran. Jodi would listen to what people were telling her yet she secretly was working on getting as strong as she possibly could.

Jodi called Robby later that day and informed him about Kevin wanting to meet in Baku.

"That's not happening Jodi," Robby responded, just as she predicted he would.

"You're going to have to get him to meet you in Turkey," Robby said.

He said he thought it most likely that Kevin was looking to meet in a Muslim country where he would feel safe. It would not make the most optimal situation, but Robby said he believed that the Turkish government would work with them, but first, they needed time to get things into place.

Time, you are my enemy and my friend.

Robby and Jodi had spoken with Donna earlier that month and the three of them had agreed that they would have just one shot ever at getting Kevin out with Mari and then to get Jodi and Mari safely back to the United States.

Jodi called Kevin on the day he had demanded her to. She told him she couldn't get a visa to Baku, which was true. She then asked him if he had thought about Turkey as a meeting spot. He said he had and that it was an easy trip for Iranians and common for his countrymen to travel there. He said he would work on the details and for Jodi to call him back in two days.

"Can I talk to Mari again?" Jodi ventured to ask.

"No," the call was disconnected.

I hadn't thought he would let me talk to her, but I felt we were getting closer and closer to getting him out of Iran with Mari.

CHAPTER 11

July/August 2011
Charlottesville, VA/Hale, MI
(The plan/Jodi returns to hometown)

Jodi called Kevin two days later as he had demanded. She felt prepared, as she had already met with Robby in his office to go over the details of potentially meeting Kevin in Turkey.

"After Kevin crosses into Turkey, he will be stopped," Robby explained. "Once the Turkish government has Mari, they will allow you to come in to Turkey so you can work with their court system to regain custody of her. Then, you'll be able to bring her home."

Robby told her that the court process, at times, could take very long to get a child out of the system.

"It can take weeks, even months," Robby added.

"Are you kidding me?" Jodi responded. Her mind couldn't comprehend what Robby was telling her. She knew that Turkey was their least favorite choice, but hearing Robby spell out the plan made the thought unimaginable.

How could her rights as a parent not apply in Turkey? Her child would not be hers? It was ludicrous to think it could be a solution. But then, what other choice was there? The world was in such chaos and Mari was being held in Iran at the epicenter of maelstrom.

"What choice do we have Robby? There isn't anything else," Jodi said with resignation, acquiescing to the new plan. She had played, "we have one shot at getting Kevin out with Mari – just one shot," over and over in her head for weeks and knew at that time it was never more true.

She really did just have one chance to lure Kevin out of Iran with Mari and only one shot at getting Mari back home.

If Kevin had any idea about what was to happen, he would never have taken one step out of Iran.

Jodi turned her attention back to her conversation with Kevin.

"Did you find out about Istanbul?" Jodi asked him, careful not to call him Hussain or Kevin. She never knew his mood or what name he wanted to be called. It was a strange way to communicate, but she could tell it was working. It was like trying to walk on eggshells, but worth the effort. The person who she loved most in the world, Mari, depended on her to be the level-headed strong mother who could accomplish anything. Hopefully she remembered.

Kevin agreed to meet in Istanbul. He said if Jodi brought him $10,000 cash, a laptop computer and a two-way radio equipped with a **GPS** system, she would be allowed to visit Mari. He made it very clear to her that she would never be alone with Mari and to not expect to take her home.

"If you prove to me that you can be a good person, I will consider if I will let Mari come home to the United States one day," Kevin pronounced. The dreaded silence began as the call was terminated.

Jodi lay in bed that night, (a bed which amounted to a single sleeping bag on the floor in the little room she rented) and stared out the window. She loved that little room. She didn't think she deserved a bed, because she didn't know if Mari had one. All around her were what belongings Mari and she had left in the world.

Jodi had sold most of their earthly possessions and even had given some away during the past two years to pay bills, lawyers and to simply survive. At that time to make money, she was working selling credit card systems business-to-business. It was a flexible job, with flexible hours and because she was a traveling salesman of sorts, none of the businesses she called on knew her or her story.

"I could go about my business of bringing Mari home."

During that period of time, Jodi knew approximately 12 people in the state of Virginia. She could name them all; two FBI agents, two lawyers and eight people she called friends, people she absolutely trusted. There were acquaintances, of course, but it was so much easier for her to stay clear of them and away from their prying and insensitive questions.

"Why haven't you gotten her home yet? Why doesn't the government go get her? Well, at least she IS with her father – right?" were the questions Jodi was asked most often.

Self-imposed isolation is nothing Jodi would recommend because it isn't healthy, but it worked for her. She had to do, what she had to do.

"Strange thoughts creep into your mind when someone you love is missing. The self-destructive guilt that you place on yourself, puts you in a dark place that very few people can understand," Jodi explained.

Kevin's words replayed in Jodi's mind as she gazed at the stars in the night sky.

If I was a good person, he would consider letting Mari come back to the states one day.

She knew, on that June night, that Kevin was not going to allow Mari to go back with her that summer. She wasn't even sure that he was going to let them visit. Jodi's mind was filled with despair as the "what if's" developed in her thoughts. What if Kevin took Mari's life?

"Would I know? Would I sense it?" she wondered.

At this point, for the first time in her life, she thought about suicide. She knew it was wrong and a sin because of her Christian faith. But then, that night, in her mind, she planned what she would do and mentally composed messages to her parents and brothers. She honestly believed that God would forgive her for her actions.

"I knew I couldn't live with the knowledge the one person that should have loved Mari as much as I did, didn't. I couldn't live with the knowledge that Mari wasn't alive and that I hadn't been able to protect her." Jodi confessed.

In the early morning hours, Jodi officially planned out her suicide, if she ever received proof that Kevin had killed their daughter. She was totally relieved when her plan was completed and she would not have to make the decision again.

Once she had worked through the details of taking her own life, she prayed again. This time she asked for help - for her Father in Heaven to penetrate Kevin's heart, to prompt him to leave Iran with Mari.

"I prayed and prayed," said Jodi.

Very early the next morning, Kevin called her. She was surprised by the call. It was quite soon since their last conversation and she hesitated with worry before she answered.

"Jojo, I want you to listen to me. I need some things before we meet. I want you to send me three shirts, very nice shirts. You know my size. I want you to send Mari a pair of sandals and I want $2,000 in cash. I need traveling money so I can meet you in Istanbul. Remember what I have told you, Jodi. I am Iranian and not the man you knew! If you want to see your daughter alive, you will do what I have said!"

My skin would crawl when he used that tone. He had become a stranger to me. A stranger who was with my daughter.

Jodi agreed to send the items and told him she would do it quickly to make sure the package would arrive before they left for Istanbul. They both agreed to use the Istanbul Hilton as a place to leave messages about where they were staying in Turkey.

"Kevin then said if I could prove that I had $10,000 for him, the computer and the other items he demanded, that he might consider travelling back to the United States with me." Jodi said.

He asked her if his permanent resident status was still valid and Jodi answered, "Yes."

"Good, because I don't want to get in trouble for leaving," Kevin said.

Jodi knew her plan was working if Kevin was worried about his status in the United States. He didn't need to know that what he perceived to be the truth was not.

On July 21, Kevin called Jodi again and began screaming.

"Do you play me for a fool? Do you think you are smarter than me?"

"What are you talking about?" Jodi screamed back.

She didn't know why he was trying to mess with her. They hadn't spoken in several weeks and she was sure he was trying to play her about meeting him in Istanbul. She had sent him the package with the money, shirts and sandals, so she was hoping that he still planned on meeting her.

"It's the 21st and your package has not arrived like I requested," Kevin said. "I kept on waiting and it has not come. You did not send it, did you?" he accused.

Starting to cry, Jodi told him that she had sent the package and gave him the tracking number provided so that he could go online and check for himself to see where it was.

"Please come to Istanbul, I need to see my baby. I need to hold Mari again. It has been over two years and Mari and I deserve to see each other," Jodi said. She knew she was pleading and crying-begging.

"Kevin, please! This is killing my father, as well. My dad is really ill and I need to let him know that you are going to at least let me see Mari. Please Kevin, you can make this happen," Jodi begged.

For several seconds, Jodi heard nothing, complete silence, but she could sense he was still on the other end of the call.

"You better not be f**** lying to me!" he yelled, before Jodi heard the call disconnected.

The end of the month was near. Jodi had earlier learned, before Kevin's burst of rage, that her father needed open heart surgery. She hadn't left Virginia for 26 months and was reluctant to; afraid to leave Donna and Robby, her links to Mari. Yet, she had done everything she could in Virginia. She was lonely and her parents needed her. Jodi knew it was time to leave.

After one year, things had changed relating to her daughter's abduction, Jodi observed. During the first few months, authorities from various agencies frequently phoned and Jodi compared it to people ringing your doorbell to deliver casseroles after the death of a loved one. They come in great numbers at first and mean well, yet it becomes overwhelming as you run out of room to put the casseroles. As time passes, the casseroles slowly stop being delivered and people move on.

"Time heals all wounds they say, but for the left behind parent and the child, who is missing, time doesn't heal the situation and they don't get to move on," Jodi described.

Jodi packed what belongings she deemed necessary and her friend Elsie placed the rest of Jodi's possessions in storage for her.

It felt so odd leaving Virginia.

Jodi had met Elsie during a job interview. They had both applied to sell timeshares at a local resort and the women hit it off right away. Elsie was an energetic, very confident and sweet redhead. She and Jodi went through training sessions together. Jodi was leery of making new friends at the time, because of not wanting to explain her situation. With Elsie, it became easy and she was soon able to confide in her.

Elsie had asked Jodi why she applied for the position and Jodi said she wanted extra income. She told her about her other job selling credit card machines. Elsie said that she too wanted extra income. She was retired but her energetic self wouldn't allow her to stay home and she loved being around people.

"She was larger than life," Jodi fondly recalled.

Elsie invited Jodi to her yoga class, which met twice a week and cost $5 each visit.

"You'll enjoy it," Elsie prodded.

Jodi thought about it and justified spending the $5, thinking it would be good for her. She had always wanted to learn yoga.

After her first session, Elsie invited her to grab a glass of wine at a local bistro. It felt good to Jodi to take a break from her routine of being alone. She thought that her new friend could sense her loneliness. During their first glass of wine, Elsie ordered a gourmet pizza for them to share and eventually, Jodi told her about Mari and everything that had brought her to living in a rented room doing odd jobs and living in Virginia with no family.

Elsie told Jodi she found her story fascinating.

The women became very close friends during Jodi's final six months in Virginia. Elsie and her husband Bill, welcomed Jodi to dinners, boat rides and helped her in every way they could. Elsie was forever coming up with ideas and she was the only other person on the earth who knew about Jodi's plan "B." Elsie told Jodi that she didn't want her to have to go, but admitted, "If it were my loved one being held in Iran, I would probably decide to do the exact same thing."

Jodi checked with the postal service before she left to make certain her package for Kevin had arrived in Iran. It had. Kevin had lied to her again and she knew it was his excuse not to leave Iran and also to get more money. It was time to finish plan "B" and get herself into that country.

"I hated not telling Robby or Donna, but I knew the feedback from them would not match my decision," said Jodi, recalling the guilt she felt.

However, she decided she would wait until her dad was out of surgery and feeling better, before she began executing her secret plan.

She notified Robby and Donna that she was going home to Michigan to see her parents through her father's surgery. Donna phoned her after she had hit the road to ask how she was doing.

Donna was a sweetheart.

The agent cared for Jodi and Mari with such devout feeling. Donna always made Jodi feel that Mari was of the utmost importance to her. She asked Jodi how she felt about Kevin cancelling the trip again.

"I feel OK, but I have a feeling that I will see Mari soon, which keeps me going," Jodi said truthfully.

"Had Donna known the truth about plan 'B,' she probably would have kicked my butt FBI style to get me to think clearly and not go to Iran by myself," Jodi admitted.

CHAPTER 12

AUG. 1-3, 2011 (MONDAY-WEDNESDAY)
HALE, MI
(PREPARATIONS)

JODI'S FATHER WAS SCHEDULED FOR triple bypass heart surgery in mid-July, so the Reed children and their families travelled to Hale, Michigan, their hometown, to be together during the ordeal. An added benefit was that they would all be in the same place for their parent's 50th wedding anniversary; however, because Mari was still being held somewhere on the other side of the world, Jodi's mom and dad told their children that they just did not feel like celebrating. The ups and downs of Kevin constantly changing plans had all of them feeling very tense.

It was the first time Jodi had seen Vern, her older brother, in more than two years. He knew very little about what had transpired since he had last seen his sister, because Jodi had not wanted to talk about it with him on the telephone. Her business with the FBI was kept among a very small circle of people.

Jodi was always concerned that information would somehow get to Kevin if she spoke to too many people. The biggest threat in her mind was that Kevin might hear there were warrants out for his arrest and that he no longer had legal custody of Mari. She had been very careful not to divulge too many details to everyone in her family because of Facebook and other social media. Her mother and youngest brother, Matt, were aware of most of what was going on at the time.

In the safety of the family home, Jodi told Vern what she could. He, like Matt, has a heart of pure gold, Jodi likes to say, and he will share anything he has with anyone who needs it.

She said Vern was shocked to hear the details of what she was going through. He told her he knew it had been bad, because he could hear the unspoken truths in his mom's voice when he called home, yet he couldn't have imagined the extent of her terror.

Jodi saw tears well in Vern's eyes as she continued to describe the past two years of her life, but ever in the role as eldest sibling, he remained solid and strong. She recited her journey, sounding extremely calm, because she had put herself in her frozen place again, and the secret place where she was planning "B." The plan kept her going, helping her to remain a functioning adult and keeping her from slipping into that dark place where she did not want to go.

Vern's world is his family. He had married the love of his life Cindee many years ago and they raised three wonderful sons. He is a happy man, busy with his church, his school and his family. He told Jodi it had been an extreme hardship for him not really knowing what was happening in her life and not seeing her for so long.

Matt and Vern tried to joke with Jodi like they had done since they were kids, yet they could feel her pain as she dialed Kevin time and time again. Still, it didn't matter that the three of them were 49, 47 and 42 years old; they loved to act goofy together.

"When we were together, we felt and acted like we were children again," Jodi laughed.

She loved being with her brothers and acting like the "Three Stooges" relieved some of the tension of their Dad's bypass surgery. Their parents would get a little weary from their rotten jokes, practical jokes and other nonsense while at the hospital and they would finally good naturedly, kick them out of the room.

There was never a time in their lives that the three Reed siblings did not feel close with each other. Yet lately, it seemed their silly reunions only took place at hospitals, as their parents battled with age-related health issues.

Her brothers saw that their "joyful, joking sister" was gone, yet she assumed her role of trying to make everyone happy around her. At other times, her family would observe her sitting sadly and staring out the window with her phone in her hand, always trying to reach Kevin.

I needed to know that Mari was OK. The pressure of knowing Dad was having a triple bypass and that he missed Mari so much was a lot of weight on my shoulders. He wanted me to have Mari home safely and be his happy daughter again.

Jodi's father sailed through surgery and doctors pronounced that he could return home to continue his recovery. She was sad to know that it was time to say goodbye to Vern and did not want him to know how much she yearned for him to stay. She knew he had to get back to his family which made her a little envious. That's all Jodi wanted, to be reunited with her family – her Mari.

Matt, Nancy and their boys stayed at the family cottage for a few days more to help their father settle in and to make sure his parents had everything they needed.

Matt and his wife had purchased the cottage several years before and had been extremely generous to share it with Jodi that summer. The three of them would spend hours talking late into the night about what could be happening with Mari and what Jodi should do next. Then, all too soon, Matt and his family left and Jodi felt an odd sense of, "What do I do now?"

"It was awful, truly awful," said Jodi. "I felt so empty and alone, even though I was next door to my parents."

She thought she should be used to the familiar loneliness she had endured since Mari had been gone. While she was with her brothers, it wasn't as harsh as it had been before. With both of her brothers now gone, even though the loneliness of life without Mari had never subsided, it hit her hard.

She tried to get her emotions under control by walking around the empty cottage. She didn't want to cry, because she would be seeing her mom and dad soon, popping in to check on them. Generally it was hard for Jodi to let people see her cry. Throughout her life, she had encountered sadness, but nothing would ever compare to the feelings she owned now, knowing first-hand what it was like to have a missing child or perhaps worse - a child who was dying or who had been killed.

"Feeling like I was going to cry all the time was something new to me," Jodi admitted.

Jodi knew that she couldn't pull anything over on her mother if she showed up with swollen eyes and a tear-stained face. Her parents needed to focus on getting her father healed, and not worry about her. She did what she found worked every time to get over the crying and loneliness – she hit the floor to do sit-ups and push-ups.

"I would do sets of 50 each. Usually two to three sets tired me enough to let go of some of the pain which led to my crying," said Jodi.

Additionally, she planned to do some serious work on her plan "B" later that night by setting dates on how to accomplish it. Thinking about actually going into Iran helped her feel closer to Mari by doing something which would bring her back home.

It was Monday, the first of August, 2011. She dialed Kevin's number, with no expectation that he would answer. Just the act of dialing had become a ritual at that point, which helped Jodi with her, "Am I doing everything possible to get Mari home," guilt.

"Hello Jojo!" answered Kevin. He sounded like the old Kevin, the man who had held Jodi's hand when they first laid eyes on their newborn daughter.

Jodi was shocked to hear his voice.

"Hello, how are you and Mari?" she asked, not certain which name to call him.

Early on, he had demanded that she call him Hussain, his birth name. When she had met him years before, she understood that he used Hussain as his middle name. She continued to talk with him cautiously, hoping to not set him off.

"Listen, Jojo. I will meet you in Istanbul, Turkey this Friday and let you visit with Mari," he said. "Mari wants to see you and I think it would be good for her. We will stay one week to 10 days. I will secure our travels and make it there by Friday, the fifth. Can you?"

Jodi was shocked to hear what he said, because she had been praying many times, every day asking God to soften Kevin's heart. She recalled that she prayed brief prayers, more like chats talking with her Heavenly Father as many as 12-15 times each day.

"I knew the power of prayer and again, it helped me with the, "Am I doing everything I can to get Mari home guilt."

Before Jodi could answer Kevin, he asked if she wanted to talk with Mari. The everyday, normal tone in his voice confused her. It was like talking to him back when he had taken Mari on one of the many daddy-daughter weekends they had taken in the past.

"Hi Mama!" greeted Mari, who sounded a bit happier since the last time they spoken.

"Hi Sweetie! How are you?"

Mari chirped she was fine and that her Baba told her he was taking her on a trip to visit her mother. Her Iranian accent was very thick, but she sounded so sweet. Jodi felt she had landed in heaven, just hearing Mari's happy voice.

"Yes, Baba has told me that. I am going to get my ticket and will meet you both there. I am looking forward to seeing you again," Jodi responded.

Jodi was choosing her words very carefully, because she could hear Kevin listening and prompting Mari.

Mother and daughter exchanged goodbyes, complete with, "I love you's," before Mari's voice faded away. Jodi sensed she wanted to keep talking, but that Baba wouldn't allow it.

Kevin got back on the phone and with a stern voice told her she had better make certain she called him the next day with her itinerary to Istanbul. "Click." No goodbye was offered before the call ended.

Jodi stood in place, frozen. Did the call really just happen? Did Kevin tell her he would meet her in Turkey on Friday? After standing in the same spot for a few minutes, other thoughts penetrated her mind. Was he tricking her? Why now? Was he really going to bring Mari?

"I was happy, scared, cautious and confused all at the same time," Jodi remembered.

Her moment was interrupted when her phone began to ring. She looked down to see who it was and saw it was an international call. She knew it was Kevin.

"Jojo, don't forget what I told you to bring; $10,000 in cash, a laptop and walkie talkies for me. If you do not, you will not see Mari again!" Kevin demanded before he hung up.

His voice was filled with darkness, a menacing tone that made the hair on Jodi's arms stand up. The memory of Mari's sweet voice faded in her mind as her thoughts went into mommy mode. Without any more thought, Jodi quickly called Robby. She couldn't get the words out fast enough.

"Robby, I just talked with Kevin. I called and he answered. He says the trip is on to Istanbul and he will meet me this Friday, on the fifth."

"How do you feel about that Jodi? Do you think this is a trick, or is he for real this time?" Robby said levelly. "This is it, our one shot at getting Mari back here."

The trip had been called off just a short time before, and now everyone who was involved had to scramble to make sure it would work. They had just one shot. Donna had called to set up airline tickets and hotels in Istanbul and to check on Jodi and to see how her father was doing. Donna told her she might not hear from Robby for a little while, as he had to get many details handled with the Turkish government. Jodi was instructed to call Donna if she had any questions and to wait to hear of news from Robby.

Donna said that the State Department, the FBI legate in Turkey, the Turkish Police, the Turkish Children's Police and Interpol, all had to be notified immediately.

Jodi called Matt after hanging up with Donna. She looked up at the clock and knew they had been on the road for about two hours.

"Matt, Kevin called and said he is going to meet me on Friday. I need you to come back and help with Mom and Dad. I'm going to get Mari!" Jodi said, out of breath from excitement.

She was six days away from seeing her daughter again. Jodi was filled with so much anticipation that she felt like she didn't weigh a single ounce, gravity wasn't holding her down. "I knew God had answered my prayers once again."

Without hesitation, Matt turned his mini-van around and headed back to their cottage.

Jodi quickly took inventory of herself. Was she prepared for the trip? She knew that she was in the best physical shape she had ever been in. Her workouts had been intense; having anticipated that she would be the one to physically rescue Mari. During the past two years, she had done excessive exercising and power training. It wasn't a normal exercise program and she wasn't sure if it was sane, but it got her through the long days and nights of missing Mari. It got her through not feeling like she had done enough that day to bring her daughter home. It got her though the guilt she had of trusting Kevin in the past. It got her out of the dark world she was living in.

She had already begun lowering her caloric intake, because she knew that if she had to travel overseas, she would not take the time to eat. She also had gradually reduced her heart and blood pressure medications to a minimum, because if she had to stay in Turkey for an extended period of time, she would not have access to her medicine. If she had to escape into Greece to get Mari out of Turkey, she was ready.

She was ready to fight for her daughter.

After confirming the details of her itinerary with Donna, Jodi called Kevin. He answered and she told him about her flight and that she was bringing all of the items he had requested. She hoped and prayed he would be in a good mood and still planned to meet her. She noted a pause before he began speaking.

"Jojo, I have tickets for our travel. We will be coming by train. We leave on Thursday and will arrive in Istanbul early Saturday morning. When are you coming?" He demanded.

"I have my flight on Friday and will arrive on Saturday as well, but in the afternoon," Jodi said, trying not to sound too anxious.

What she had told Kevin was a lie, but she was getting good at being able to stay calm and focused at what was at play. Her tickets were set for Sunday because, according to Turkish laws, she physically could not be in Turkey until Mari was separated from her father and placed in an orphanage.

Kevin told Jodi that he would call her when they left on Thursday, because once they crossed over into Turkey, his Iranian cell phone wouldn't work. He said that he would meet her at the Hilton in Istanbul on Saturday afternoon.

No mention of Mari

"Have a safe flight, Jojo," then she heard nothing more.

"I knew what his kind words of 'having a safe flight' meant. He wanted what I was bringing him and nothing more," Jodi said.

The next few days were a blur as Robby and Donna continue to help Jodi prepare for her time in Istanbul. There were several documents requiring her signature. Jodi received them all by mail and was responsible for getting them notarized and returned by overnight delivery.

Matt, Nancy and the boys remained with Jodi. They told her it felt like they were all in a "Lifetime" movie, with so much action and drama going on. The adults were taking notes about everything as it happened. All of them were praying that the trip wasn't a trick Kevin was plotting.

Their understanding from the numerous phone calls was that once Kevin and Mari crossed into Turkey, the Turkish police would arrest Kevin for international parental kidnapping. Mari would then be placed into the hands of the Turkish Children's Police, who would then place her into their social system and protect her until Jodi's arrival.

CHAPTER 13

AUGUST 3, 2011
HALE, MI
(WHERE'S KEVIN?)

THE AFTERNOON OF AUG. 3, Robby called Jodi and told her he had some news that would be hard to hear, but not to worry, because everything would be worked out.

"This isn't what we wanted to hear Jodi, but it is how it is going to happen. Kevin will not be arrested in Turkey, but the plan to separate him from Mari will still take place," Robby firmly reported.

Jodi could sense from his tone that there was more to the story, but that would be all he would tell her at the time. She had learned over the past two years when to ask more questions and when not to, just by listening to the tone of his voice.

"Robby, you just signed my death warrant," Jodi contended.

Kevin would now know that for two years I had planned this; that I lied to him and lured him out of Iran. Mari will be in an orphanage and Kevin would be running around free in Istanbul while I'm supposed to walk the streets of the city and orchestrate Mari's release.

Yeah, that's going to work out well.

After hanging up with Robby - Matt, Nancy and Jodi began bouncing ideas off of each other trying to figure out what to do. Matt said he was angry at the thought of Jodi being alone in an unfamiliar country with Kevin planning to do who knows what, fully knowing he was tricked in being separated from Mari.

"How did this happen?" burst out Nancy, "Why did you guys pick Turkey? Why didn't they tell you before he wouldn't be arrested?"

Jodi felt calm; having been through this type of experience many times during the past two years. She wasn't surprised in the least. She was upset however, knowing what Kevin would do about what he would see as a betrayal.

I knew he would kill me in Istanbul.

She thought it funny to know that, and not be very upset. She reminded herself that Kevin was a man she had never really known. His actions the past two years validated her feelings of knowing what he was capable of doing.

So, Matt, Nancy and Jodi all agreed that she should call the meeting with Kevin off.

"I was heartbroken, but I knew I was no good to my daughter if I were dead and she, in turn, would never get her life back," Jodi thought. She dialed Robby and Matt took the phone away from his sister.

"Robby, this is Matt. I need to talk to you about what you told my sister about Kevin not being arrested in Turkey. I don't think that is at all safe for her to travel to Istanbul with Kevin on the loose. This is not the same guy we all knew," Matt began.

He continued to tell Robby that the man he thought he knew would never have taken Mari away from Jodi. However, after the abduction everything changed and he had witnessed calls from Kevin and the threats he made concerning his niece and his sister.

"We have been talking and wondering if we should call the meeting off with him before he gets to the Turkish border. Tell him Jodi couldn't get through customs because of the large amount of money she was carrying, then work to force him out once again to a different country, one that will arrest him," Matt told the agent.

Jodi could see Matt restraining his anger while talking to Robby. However, he knew Jodi trusted Robby completely, which made it easier for Matt to work at trusting him as well.

"Let me think about this, Matt and get back to you. Please tell Jodi to stay calm and that we will get through this. I'll call you back as soon as I know something. Tell her I'm also upset about the arrest warrant being lifted," Robby said.

Shortly after Matt spoke with Robby, Jodi's phone rang and she saw it was Kevin. He was still in Iran. She had studied the train route from Tehran to Istanbul and knew by counting the hours how long it would take for them to reach the border before losing phone contact.

Jodi softly said, "Hello?" hesitant to find out why he was calling.

"Hello Mama!"

It was Mari! Jodi's heart raced as well as the thoughts in her brain, making her head hurt. Where was she? Why is she calling me now? Had Kevin cancelled the trip again?

"I am on a train coming to see you," Mari said, in her grown up voice.

Jodi began to relax as she knew with certainty that the plan was in motion. The thought made her feel very strong.

I knew, no matter what, that I was going to Turkey to get my daughter.

Kevin took the phone from Mari and told Jodi that they were on the train. He informed her that he expected to lose cell service in about an hour and that Mari wanted to talk with her.

"I will put her back on so she can visit with you. I will see you in Istanbul. Remember our plan," he said briskly.

Mari returned to the phone and Jodi could hear Kevin speaking in Farsi in the background. Jodi knew she just had a few precious moments to speak to Mari.

"Mari, let's play a game."

"OK."

"What color is the sky?"

"Blue," she quickly said.

"That's right! That's the color of mommy's eyes."

Mari giggled and the game continued with Jodi asking about the color of a tree.

"Brown!"

"That's right and that is the color of mommy's hair. It is longer now than you remember, so I will have brown hair and blue eyes when you see me."

Jodi was certain that Mari had not seen any photos of her in more than two years and because she now was only eight years old, she didn't think Mari would remember what she looked like. She didn't want to frighten her when they were reunited.

She asked her what the color of grass was and Mari correctly answered green. Jodi laughed and said, "That's right, you are so smart! That is also the color of frogs." Jodi was rewarded by hearing another of Mari's little girl giggles.

Jodi could still hear Kevin talking in the background and knew she was safe playing her game with Mari.

"What color are Mari's eyes?" Jodi asked.

"Brown."

"What color is Mari's hair?"

"Brown."

Mother and daughter spoke for approximately 30 minutes, the longest stretch of time since she had left for Tehran. Mari's accent was very heavy, but she sounded so good to Jodi. Mari said she was excited to be on the train and described what she saw outside her window.

Then she blurted out, "Baba says that if you are a good person, I might be able to see you again one day,"

Her words struck Jodi like lightening from the sky, piercing her soul. She wasn't sure if Mari meant she would be able to see her on this trip, or if he was preparing her not to see Jodi ever again.

"Mommy is a good person, Sweetie; we will see each other soon. Mommy loves you with all of her heart."

"I have to go now Mama, Baba says it is time to hang up the phone."

"OK Sweetie, I love you very much and you have fun riding the train."

"I love you too, Mama."

Jodi believed that she and Mari had been able to talk for so long because Kevin had been engaged in another conversation. Jodi slowly hung up the phone and realized that Matt and Nancy had been sitting quietly together just watching her. Nancy asked how she was doing and Jodi said she was fine.

"That was the longest I have been able to talk with Mari," she said, beginning to tear up. She stopped the tears from falling, because she knew that she must stay in control. She calmed herself down by holding on to the sound of Mari's voice in her head.

Matt shook his head at Jodi.

"How do you know how to handle things, like getting her to play the game of remembering you?" he asked.

"I pray all of the time to ask God for the answers. It comes to me with the "Mommy Power" He gives me," Jodi answered.

Matt grinned that special smile that he reserves for his sister.

Jodi called Robby to tell him that she had just talked with Mari and that Kevin said they were about an hour from losing his cell service. Jodi thought that they must be close to the Iranian/Turkish border, but she wasn't positive. Robby told her he was still actively working on what to do. He said he would call her shortly to tell her whether or not to cancel the meeting or to continue with their plan.

"You're doing great Jodi, just hang in there!" he encouraged.

The afternoon passed quietly, as Jodi wasn't interested in talking. She just wanted to hold the sound of Mari's voice inside her head, while praying for her safety. Nancy had taken Luke and Jake uptown to pick up supplies for dinner. Matt had gone to their parent's house to give them an update and to check on their dad. After a couple of hours, Matt, Nancy and the boys joined Jodi at "Mari Headquarters" again.

Jodi looked at her caller ID when her phone rang. It was Robby to tell her if she would be going to Turkey. Jodi didn't even have time to say, "Hello," before Robby started talking.

"We have them, we have Mari! She is fine and they are in Van, Turkey!" His voice was happy, excited and confident. Jodi's heart was bursting with joy but her head demanded logic and she found herself asking Robby a barrage of questions.

"How is she? What is happening with Kevin? Is she safe from harm?" The questions continued rolling off her tongue.

Robby said that everything was fine and that Kevin was in police headquarters talking with a prosecutor as to why they were holding Mari.

"Mari is in another area, away from Kevin," Robby explained.

He told her that a State Department representative would be calling her and that he too would call Jodi once he received another update. Again he urged her to "keep hanging in there."

Soon, a woman named Lisa from the State Department in Ankara, Turkey, phoned Jodi to tell her that her daughter had been removed from her father and about how Mari would be transported to a facility in Istanbul the very next morning. Jodi also heard of how Mari and Kevin had been traveling under false names and were not on the train's manifest, and how police identified them from photographs.

"They confirmed Mari's identity by locating the tiny mole behind her ear that you told them about," Lisa said excitedly.

She told Jodi that they would have Mari call her once they reached her and assured Jodi everything was going to be fine. Jodi was instructed to get to Turkey as quickly as possible to start the legal work to get Mari home. Jodi thanked Lisa for all she was doing, hung up the phone and allowed herself to break down and cry.

I was within hours and days of seeing Mari and she was finally out of Iran – the only place on earth that I couldn't travel to as a U.S. citizen.

Suddenly, a bad feeling washed over Jodi and she told Matt that something was wrong. She didn't know what it was, but it was a feeling deep in her gut.

CHAPTER 14

AUGUST 4, 2011
HALE, MI
(WHERE'S MARI?)

A FEW HOURS HAD PASSED when Robby rang Jodi again.

"How are you doing Jodi?" he asked, this time sounding way too serious.

Jodi stood up to look outside the window.

"I'm the same, really. Just waiting to hear about what's happening."

"Are Matt and Nancy still with you?" Robby began.

Something was wrong. I could hear it in his voice.

"Just tell me Robby."

She turned her attention to where Matt and Nancy were. Matt was sitting, reading a newspaper, trying to look busy and Nancy was in the kitchen getting lunch together.

"Yes, they're both right here. Robby, tell me what's wrong," she urged, staring wide-eyed at her brother who looked up at her.

Levelly, Robby instructed Jodi to sit down and not to get too upset with what he was about to tell her. He continued to tell her why in a low voice.

"Something went wrong at the prosecutor's office." Robby explained to Jodi that the prosecutor had told Kevin that Jodi had filed criminal charges against him and that was the reason why Mari had been separated from him. The prosecutor in Van didn't believe that the charges were still valid, because he didn't know about any requests to arrest him.

"He released Mari back into Kevin's custody," Robby reported.

"I was as devastated as a human being could possibly be," Jodi said.

By that time, Matt and Nancy had moved closer to her. Jodi could barely breathe as she thought that it was very possible that she would never see her daughter again. Then, the realization set in that Kevin would probably hurt Mari for what Jodi had done.

Jodi began pacing in the living room, willing air to enter her lungs.

"I couldn't breathe."

She looked at Matt who saw the fear on her face.

"I can't listen to this anymore!" Jodi cried, as she flung her phone at Matt. She made her way around the corner of the kitchen and out the back door. As she stumbled outside, she felt her chest pounding so fast and hard that she thought she was going to have a heart attack.

With her right fist she punched the wall of the cottage over and over until her hand bled and one knuckle was broken, if not two. She couldn't feel the pain and just kept walking. Jodi said she felt frozen like never before. So cold. The sun hit her and although it was a very warm summer day, she just felt cold.

Her heart was breaking and all she could think was that Kevin and Mari were going to go back to Iran and that she would never see or hold her little girl again.

Jodi stumbled up to an apple tree that had grown in the backyard for years and reached up above her head to grasp a branch to hang on to.

"Please, God, please don't let me have a heart attack. I need to get to Mari," Jodi prayed.

Blood from her hand was running down her arm, which caught her attention and snapped her back to reality.

"Tell me – no! Show me what to do!" Jodi screamed towards Heaven.

A little brown Wren landed between her hands on the limb and just looked at her. What seemed like minutes, but was mere seconds, the little bird and Jodi were part of a staring contest. Her heart began to beat steadily once again as she kept eye contact with the unmoving bird and she was warmed by the comfort that God had blessed her. Her heart filled with the knowledge that everything would work out.

"Thank you Lord, I understand," she whispered.

A week before, a baby Wren had fallen from its nest and had broken its wing on a cement slab just outside the front door of the cabin. Jodi watched and waited for a time to see if its mother would return. When she didn't, Jodi took "Zeus" inside and made a nest for him in an old fish tank she had found stored in a closet.

The baby Wren acted like it loved being "mothered" by Jodi, yet she knew more than just his wing was injured. She would see him hopping around his little caged area and she would also place him on the floor, sitting with the fledgling and watching him hop around.

"I loved feeling needed."

She cried after Zeus lived only three more days. She had hoped to save him for Mari, as Mari would have loved the little bird. Jodi had named the wren Zeus, because the mythical God was known as the Lord of the Sky, just like Zeus was to Jodi.

Matt had followed his sister outside and was keeping his distance as he continued to talk with Robby. Matt had heard Jodi punch the wall and had watched her become ghostly white. She looked like all of the blood had drained away from her face. The life that she had been anticipating beginning again had just been swept away from her. She turned and approached Matt then. While still listening to Robby, Matt mouthed, "Are you OK?"

"Let me talk to Robby – I'm OK," Jodi said, reaching for her phone.

"Jodi wants to talk to you again, Robby." Matt put his hand over the phone so Robby couldn't hear him.

"Don't freak out on him. He's trying to tell us what to do and how sorry he is about what's happening," Matt said it firmly but with kindness.

Matt could tell that her thoughts were out of control, because of the crazy look in her eyes. She was not quite focused on him. The bleeding from her knuckles had stopped and he saw dark blood crusted on her hand. She still couldn't feel any pain but her hand was beginning to swell. Matt moved to look at it and reached to hold it so he could see it more closely. Jodi shook his advance away, telling him that she didn't give a crap about her hand.

I didn't give a crap about anything in the entire world at that moment, but finding out how Mari was doing. It was the first time in two years and three months that I didn't know where my daughter was.

"Robby, he will hurt her now, I just know it. He is going to head back into Iran and I will never see Mari again. He's going to pass his anger at me onto Mari, I can feel it. Please Robby, you have to get the Turkish authorities to help me get to her before that happens," Jodi said, voicing her worst fear.

Robby remained calm and explained that they were doing everything they could to find out where Kevin took Mari after the two left police headquarters.

Turkey had just broken the Hague Convention Agreement with the U.S.A.

Robby was still talking, but what he was saying was not setting well with Jodi. She kept trying to make Robby understand what she knew would happen and again lost control of her emotions.

She screamed at her agent; the only other person whom she believed would do anything to help her get to Mari.

"I don't care about this prosecutor's mistake; I don't care about the Hague Convention. I want to know where my daughter is! Somebody, somewhere in this world must know!" Jodi screamed.

Matt moved in line of Jodi's vision and was motioning for her to calm down. "Please, Jodi, calm down," he repeated again and again. Once more Jodi threw the phone at her brother.

"I can't do this," she sobbed. "Talk to Robby and try to get him to understand."

Matt took the phone, and after one long look into his sister's eyes, calmly interpreted Jodi's tirade, talking with Robby about the imminent threats against Mari. Robby, hearing Jodi's crying, kept asking Matt if she was OK. Matt assured him that she was tough, that she would get through it.

Matt's attention bounced between Jodi and Robby as he was willing Jodi to calm herself. He thought her reaction was uncharacteristic for his sister, but was just a tiny bit relieved to know Jodi could still feel something.

Jodi looked so pale that Matt motioned for his wife to check on her. Nancy moved closer to Jodi and placed her hand gently on her shoulder. The simple act of being touched, feeling Nancy's hand, was enough to bring Jodi out of the state she was in.

Jodi could finally see through her hazy emotions, recognized the fear for what it was and worked very hard to become rational. Matt had hung up with Robby and started talking with Jodi. He told her that Robby had assured him that everyone involved in Mari's rescue were taking the threats from Kevin very seriously and that Mari's safety was of their utmost priority.

"Matt didn't have to give me a lecture. I was feeling terrible, the one person that I believed really cared if Mari was back home was Robby and I just blew up at him like a psycho. I knew I had to call him to apologize," Jodi said.

Matt studied her gaze and made her promise him three times that she would not explode again. He reminded her she needed to take care of herself for Mari.

Nancy had gathered warm water and cloths and was trying to nurse Jodi's bruised and broken hand. Jodi thought Nancy was acting like a saint and kept telling her to not worry about it. Nancy insisted Jodi needed to have her hand checked out. Jodi looked down at her hand, which had swollen to twice its size, and didn't care.

"It doesn't hurt, Nancy. Believe me," Jodi said, trying to convince her.

Nothing in the world hurt as much as not knowing where Mari was and wondering if she was safe.

The tension in the air was thick and no one knew what to do. Matt went next door to tell their parents what had happened. Jodi assured him she was OK and to go on to give their folks an update. She walked outside. It was the only place she felt she could breathe; she needed to pray.

Seconds changed to minutes and minutes changed to hours. Her phone was ringing and Jodi saw that the call was from an Iranian exchange. She received several more calls from Iranian exchanges and let them all go to voice mail. She retrieved the messages and determined that they were from Kevin's family in Tehran, speaking in Farsi.

"Jodi, where are Mari and Kevin? What have you done with them?" was one message, much like the others. The voices in the messages sounded concerned, but Jodi didn't understand what they meant. Had Kevin called them?

The FBI advised Jodi not to answer the Iranian calls, so she continued to let the calls go to voice mail. They told her they were looking for Kevin and didn't know if he had gotten back on a train to Iran at that point.

Kevin must have called his family to tell them about what happened, Jodi decided. It was devastating to her. Over the past two years and three months, she had known that Mari was in Iran and had at least had some contact with her. Now she didn't know where her daughter was. She wondered if Kevin was taking Mari back to Iran and if he was, she knew she would never see her again.

Would Kevin follow through on his threats and dispose of her? He had been using her as a tool to get money making it clear that "love for his daughter" did not motivate his actions anymore.

It was the first time in months that Jodi's suicide plan crept back into her mind. Thinking of the bad things that could be happening to Mari was more than she could bear.

The hours passed and the gloom pervaded the house like a plague. It was eerily quiet. Jodi sat and rocked in her chair holding her phone and Mari's little pink blanket and the tiny T-shirt she had worn after she was born. The blanket and shirt still smelled of baby.

Since the summer of 2009 when Mari did not return home, Jodi had slept with the precious items under her pillow and took them everywhere she went, including meetings with the FBI and the State Department. The blanket and t-shirt were always there to bring her luck, folded up inside her purse or briefcase.

Nancy had taken the boys uptown to get them away for a bit and to explain to them what all the drama was about. Before they left, they asked Jodi if she wanted a milkshake or something, because they planned to stop to get some ice cream. Jodi smiled at this, proud to know that her nephews were so caring and had such a great mother. Jodi managed another smile at the family and said, "No, thank you." She just needed a few moments alone to pray.

Matt was devastated for his sister and didn't know what to do. He needed to use up his pent up anger and energy. He told Jodi he was going to work out and straighten up the basement at their mom and dad's house. He was frustrated at his inability to help his sister and niece.

He went down to the basement and started to let out steam by using the weights that he and his father shared. He began cleaning, power cleaning as he called it, along with his power work out. He had turned on the radio really loud, to match the amount of energy he was expending. He paused the cleaning and working out as he began talking to God, the only thing he knew he could do to help. A song came on the radio; "Mother and Child Reunion," by Paul Simon. Matt stopped everything he was doing and just listened:

No I would not give you false hope
On this strange and mournful day
But the mother and child reunion

Is only a motion away, oh, little darling of mine
I can't for the life of me
Remember a sadder day
I know they say let it be
But it just don't work out that way
And the course of a lifetime runs
Over and over again …

Matt knew it was a sign from God to him. He started out to tell his sister about it. As he approached the cabin, he could hear Jodi talking and picked up his pace to get inside. Matt looked to see his sister turn and look at him. He said the look on her face was nearly magical. She had a glow about her he had never seen before.

"They have located Mari! She and Kevin are heading towards Istanbul. They didn't go back to Iran and everyone is still working on getting to her!" Jodi said, while still on the phone.

Matt quickly figured out she was talking with Robby. Jodi put the call on speaker to let Matt listen in. Together, they heard that Kevin and Mari had been spotted on the train. Mari appeared physically OK, but was obviously very scared. Kevin was visibly upset and angry. Robby would not tell her how they knew, but it was true. Mari and Kevin were on their way to Istanbul! Jodi's and Matt's prayers had been answered.

CHAPTER 15

AUGUST 5, 2011; 2:30 A.M.
ISTANBUL, TURKEY

MATT AND JODI WERE SITTING in the living room of the cottage. She was rocking in a rocking chair. It was her way of pacing. Matt was reading an Archie comic book. Jodi remembers looking over at him and chuckling to herself, thinking back to all the years they had read about Archie and his pals. While he read, Jodi just rocked as she stared out of the picture window, rehearsing Farsi and Turkish phrases and words over and over again. The sun was getting lower in the sky, but it wouldn't yet be fully dark until after 10 o'clock.

One of the many things Jodi says she enjoys about praying is the different ways it can be done. Prayers did not always have to be spoken out loud, a lot of the time, she simply conversed with God silently. She enjoyed these conversations and always listened for His answers.

It helped Jodi pass through many, many lonely times.

That evening, Jodi's continual prayer was to keep Mari safe until she could get to her.

Matt and Nancy had finally convinced Jodi to put ice on her swollen hand. The ice made the skin sting even worse and the pain from the broken knuckles was horrific. Still, she refused to leave to go have it checked.

At 7:30 p.m. (2:30 a.m. in Istanbul) Robby called Jodi.

"We have her Jodi - we have Mari! She is safe and doing fine!" Robby exclaimed before she could even say hello. His voice sounded so different than it had been during the past few days. He was obviously relieved and excited. When she had seen the number flash on her phone, she placed it on the coffee table between herself and Matt. She had promised her brother that she would not "freak out" on Robby again. She knew that placing the phone so they both could hear pleased Matt.

"People from the State Department are on their way to be with Mari at the police station to begin the procedure," Robby continued. He said that an FBI legate in Istanbul was on his way to make sure that Mari was being protected while in custody.

"We have her Jodi!" Robby exclaimed again.

Jodi hung her head in disbelief and started to cry with relief.

"Jodi. Jodi! Are you there?" Robby asked.

"She's here Robby. She just needs a moment," Matt calmly said, not taking his eyes off of her.

Nancy came and wrapped her arms around Jodi, which made the tears flow even faster. Jodi knew she had to stop crying to talk with Robby, but it was easier said than done. Every emotion from elation to horror were tumbling around in her mind. Mari was safe, yet Kevin had to be viciously angry. Thankfully Mari was in protective custody but she had to depend on strangers to keep her safe.

"I was half way around the world from her. Mari was rescued. I had to get to her," Jodi knew.

"The official at the State Department will have her on the phone with you soon, Jodi. Hang in there, it is all going to work out," Robby said, as he ended the call.

I knew that this time, for some reason, mistakes wouldn't be made. I could feel that my daughter was safe for the first time since she left.

Matt, Nancy and Jodi walked over to their parent's home to share the good news. Nancy held her up as they walked, arm and arm. Matt kept turning his head to check on the women. He couldn't seem to slow his steps down.

"I just can't believe it; I am going to bring Mari home. I can't believe I'm going to see her again," Jodi kept saying to Nancy.

"I know, I know," Nancy responded soothingly.

After they gave their parents the news, Matt dialed Vern's number.

"They have Mari! She's safe," Matt excitedly told Vern. Jodi heard a pause and then heard Matt say that she would be heading to Istanbul the next day. Another pause.

"No, Kevin won't be in custody, but Jodi is going. Nothing will stop her." He listened to what his brother was asking and replied.

"I know, but there is no way anyone can go with her, it's too late to make the arrangements."

Before he could say anymore, Jodi told him to tell Vern that she was fine.

"Tell him I'm fine. No worries. I'll be ok in Turkey," Jodi instructed Matt.

Matt hadn't realized that Jodi could hear Vern and asked if she wanted to talk to him. She shook her head no. She said she knew if she heard his voice, she would start crying all over again. She hated to cry, always has.

The family was passing out hugs and crying about the news. Everyone was estatic that Mari had been rescued, but then reality caught up with them. They knew it meant that Jodi would be traveling to Istanbul alone to rescue Mari from an orphanage. The moment of happiness was dampened as they developed concerns about Jodi's trip.

At this point, I honestly can say I didn't have any concerns, except for Mari's safety.

Jodi knew she needed to talk with Donna. She would be the one that could make everyone understand how she was feeling about Mari's safety.

Following two and a half long grueling hours, Jodi's phone rang. She looked at the incoming call and could see that it was coming from Turkey.

"Could it be my Mari? My rescued Mari?" Jodi hoped.

Before then, calls had come to her from Iran every 30 minutes. She had changed her ring tone to alert her to those calls and every time the phone rang, everyone in the room would tense up.

"It was obvious that Kevin had called his family in Iran and told them to keep calling me," said Jodi.

She listened to all of the messages and his family sounded kind, yet it was obvious they knew.

"Why are you doing this, Jodi?" "Why is Mari taken from her father?" What happened?"

Jodi sensed they didn't know about Kevin's demands for Jodi to pay him so she would be allowed to talk to Mari. She also didn't believe they knew about all of the money and items he wanted.

Finally a call was coming in from a different number, not from Iran.

"Hello Jodi, this is Lisa with the State Department. We have a little girl here that is dying to talk with you."

Lisa explained that she was with Mari at that very moment and would stay with her through her doctor's appointment at the hospital, a necessary procedure to make sure she was healthy before she was put into an orphanage. Jodi was hanging on to every single word she spoke. Her heart was pounding fast and hard as she listened to Lisa tell her how Mari was reacting to the situation.

"I see my colleague is bringing Mari to the phone now. Please don't worry Jodi, we will watch out for her while you're traveling here. Have a safe flight and after she's checked in to the orphanage, we can have her call you again. We know your flight times, so we can make it work," Lisa said.

"Please, please don't let Kevin near her. He has threatened to kill her in the past and I'm not sure what he'll do now that she has been removed from him twice," Jodi pleaded.

Jodi was assured by Lisa that where Mari was going, was very safe and that the people in charge were prepared for her arrival and that they knew what was happening.

"Hello?" said a small, tired voice. Mari was mumbling.

"Hi Mari, this is Mommy. . ."

CHAPTER 16

AUGUST, 2011
HALE, MI
(DETAILS...)

JODI WAS HEADED TO TURKEY in just 20 hours and she had much that needed to be done. "Mommy Power" kicked in, just as it always had when she needed it the most. With astounding clarity she knew what she had to do to prepare to get Mari out of the orphanage, away from Kevin and back to the U.S. She told her brother and sister-in-law, that because Mari was in Turkey, she wouldn't know what she would have to deal with until she was there. All she could do was deal with Turkish law and Kevin, as it happened. Her family told her again how concerned they were about her going by herself.

Their worries did not affect my decisions at all. I knew I was either going to die in Turkey or bring my daughter home. In my mind there was no other choice to make.

She reminded her family that she would have the help of an attorney she had hired in Turkey. She told them that the FBI had arranged to put her up in a hotel, which they knew to be safe and would provide her with transportation when she arrived. Yet, what if their worst fears happened and she did not make it back to the United States?

"I need to ask you guys something," Jodi said to Matt and his wife. They were sitting side-by-side on the couch as Jodi paced in front of them. She couldn't make herself sit, anticipating the events of the next day.

"I think with the situation with Kevin and with my health not being the best, I want to know that if something happens to me, that both of you, I mean, I want," Jodi began.

As she stammered, trying to get the right words out, she could tell that they knew what she was about to ask. "In case something bad happens to me, I need you to finish getting Mari home and raise her as your own," she finally managed to vocalize.

Jodi needed to know that they would carry on in her absence. She needed to be sure that Mari would be in a good home and would be loved if Kevin did what she believed he was setting out to do – to get his hands on the cash and other items he wanted and then eliminate Jodi from his life, permanently,

"Of course we will," said Nancy softly and without hesitation. Matt said nothing as he kept staring at his sister. She knew it was killing him to let her go alone. Jodi thought of how proud he must be of his wife for jumping in without asking him, but the seriousness of what would be happening settled deep inside of Matt.

Robby, Donna and Jodi had already agreed that information would be passed from them to Matt and Nancy while Jodi was in Istanbul. Both agents had spoken with the couple on the phone and assured them that they would continually provide them with updates. Robby and Donna listened to their concerns and were truly amazing in dealing with her family. The agents were on the phone with all of them nonstop for 48 hours, planning and making certain they knew what to expect.

"I truly believed that they wanted Mari home as much as I did. I thanked God for them every day during my journey to get my daughter and I continue to be thankful for them and keep them in my prayers," Jodi said.

Jodi, with her family, prepared the papers which gave her brother and sister-in-law authorization to raise Mari. A close friend of Jodi's parents was a notary and was asked if she could come to their house to notarize the documents. Darlene was more aware of the situation than most people and promptly came. She wanted no explanation about the documents and was happy to be of help. Darlene is a kind and caring lady, who is a pillar of the same church as Jodi's family. Jodi had known and respected Darlene her entire life.

Darlene, like many of the people in their small community, knew that Mari had been abducted and was missing. They, of course, knew few of the details but sent cards and letters to the Reeds to pass on to Jodi, all filled with words of encouragement, love and strength.

The family minister Pastor Dave visited Jodi's parents at home sometime during the second year of Mari's absence and asked them for a fabric item of some sort, that had special meaning. After much thought, Marilyn found a hand crocheted doily, made by her grandmother. It was very old and very precious. Later that week, they met the minister at the church where they prayed together over the doily that he had anointed with oil from the Holy land. "It was lacy and pretty; designed to go on the back of a chair," Jodi described.

Pastor Dave, whom Jodi had never met, told the Reeds that he wanted Jodi to place it on her throat while she slept to promote the healing of her cancer and to give her strength.

When Jodi received the doily in the mail she felt overwhelmed with the kindness and faith it represented, not only for her but for her parents. She held it in her hands as she sent up a thank you prayer. Instead of wearing it, however, she placed it under her pillow with Mari's little blanket and outfit. She wanted to save it to give to her daughter.

"The guilt of what had happened with Mari was still weighing very heavily on me and I didn't think I deserved that beautiful item, so I saved it."

When Jodi was choosing which items to take with her to Istanbul to help Mari remember her past, Jodi put the doily on a little bear Mari had named Daffodil. Mari had earned custody of Daffodil from the American Cancer Society for selling daffodils at a spring charity function. The radio station Jodi worked for covered the event that year. Mari loved that little bear, because it had a yellow daffodil embroidered on the bottom of its little foot. Mari told her mother she didn't want to take it with her to Iran because Daffodil was supposed to stay with her mom to take care of her.

While Jodi was reflecting on the memory, she carefully tucked the bear into her brief case along with other small toys she was taking to Mari.

CHAPTER 17

Sunday, Aug. 7, 2011
JFK International Airport, New York, NY
(Next stop – Istanbul)

WAITING FOR HER CONNECTING FLIGHT to Istanbul was an exercise in frustration for Jodi. An hour after the plane's scheduled departure, Jodi finally heard her flight announced. It was time to board! First class ticket holders, families with small children, people who needed extra time boarded and then finally, coach passengers were allowed to embark.

She walked towards the plane on an elevated ramp and had to pause for a brief time as people in front of her entered the plane. She was greeted by a stewardess who smiled at her and asked if she needed help in finding her seat.

"No thank you, I'm good," Jodi responded, joining the slow walk to the back of the huge aircraft. She discovered she was just six rows from the rear bathrooms and assigned to a seat in the middle section of a row. She felt a sense of relief knowing she was finally on her way.

Thoughts were coming to her even faster than her heart was racing. She wondered if the plane's body was riveted together well and if it had enough fuel to make it across the Atlantic Ocean. She smiled as she entertained those thoughts and wondered if she was losing her mind. She found her seat after slowing her steps, waiting for people who were obviously not in a hurry to locate their own seats and store their carry-on luggage in the overhead compartments.

Jodi looked up and noticed a man sitting in the back row typing on his laptop. Above the stranger's head were numbers which could be illuminated. Jodi guessed correctly that they were there to tell flight stewards which passenger might need their help.

For some inexplicable reason, Jodi kept turning to look at the rows of numbers on the cabin wall. The fourth time she glanced back, the man's eyes connected with hers.

"I thought he was probably an FBI agent or an air marshal, having already been seated so far back before the rest of us," Jodi said. She imagined he thought she was nuts.

No one sat next to Jodi, although other rows in the cabin were filled with passengers. A pocket of space surrounded her except for three men who sat in front of her and two behind her. She assumed them to be agents.

As she settled in her seat, she did not find comfort in thinking agents were keeping tabs on her; too many mistakes had already been made and no one could protect her from Kevin if he decided to harm or kill her. Jodi believed him capable of doing either.

Before the plane took off, Jodi closed her phone and shut it off for the first time in 27 months. Doing so scared her, spinning her into a mild panic attack. Her phone was her connection to everything important to her. She slept with it close by her head and when she showered, she made sure it was close enough so she could hear it ring. She chose her clothing by making sure her phone could be carried on her person while she worked. She had not been without it since Mari had left for Iran.

Jodi was relieved as she felt the plane became airborne. She tried to settle in for the long flight, but she found it hard to sit still and kept thinking and fidgeting.

"I honestly thought I would crawl out of my skin with anxiety while getting there."

13 hours Mari, 13 hours until we are in the same country.

Whenever flight attendants brought her food, she accepted it gratefully, as it gave her something to do. She began writing a letter to her daughter in the journal she had brought along and was interrupted when a flight attendant asked if she wanted something to drink. The interruption didn't bother Jodi at all; it was a comforting distraction from worrying about Mari and praying and practicing Turkish and Farsi phrases. There was a sense of peace because she was finally sitting on the plane with the plan in motion. All of the studying would be put to practice - the waiting was finally over.

CHAPTER 18

AUGUST 8, 2011
SOMEWHERE OVER THE ATLANTIC OCEAN
(LETTER TO MARI)

Dear Mari,
    My head feels like it is so full of information that my brain actually hurts. I can't believe I am on a plane bound for Istanbul to get you, to be able to see you; touch you. I am having a hard time comprehending it. I feel like I am dreaming this and I don't want to wake up to find out it isn't true. It has been 795 days since I have seen you and looked into that silly little beautiful face. 795 days since I have been able to hold you in my arms and thank God you were born my daughter.
    I feel so bad for Uncle Matt. He and Aunt Nancy and the boys took me to the airport to fly to Istanbul and it was hard for him to send me alone. Every time I turned a corner in the people maze to go to security, he was there. I kept giving him my best "Everything Will Be Fine Smile." I had mastered it during the last 795 days. Your uncle knows me very well and he is counting on me bringing us both home safely. I signed the documents that if something happens to me in Istanbul, Uncle Matt and Aunt Nancy will raise you until you reach adult hood. I know if I can't, Uncle Matt will get you out of Istanbul and back home to America.
    It was so great hearing your voice before I boarded- my little good luck charm. I feel your anxiety about being in the orphanage and I feel your

overwhelming pain of being picked up by the police in Turkey and then released back to your father. I can only imagine what is spinning in that little head of yours. You sound good and I can hear in your voice that you are excited to see me. I loved that you asked me to put Junior, your pet frog, in my pocket and bring him to you. It's hard to imagine that your Father would not let us talk about your pets all this time. So far no one is sitting next to me, but a couple of men are looking at me. I imagine they could be air-marshals or FBI, I really don't know. I believe a lot of people know I am on this flight to get you. This "Mommy Power" that God has blessed me with is amazing. I feel stronger physically and mentally then I have in my life and I know it is His doing. If something happens to me Sweetie, please know how much I love you and I will always be with you.

Love,
Mommy

CHAPTER 19

Istanbul flight

Jodi prayed aloud about her need to have the plane land safely and for Kevin's heart to be softened, so he would do the right thing and not harm her or Mari.

She often prayed out loud, a practice she had begun after Mari was taken. Jodi guesses the reason being how lonely she felt, having had to spend so much time alone. She had become aware that people often watched her and probably judged her behavior.

She felt like she couldn't join social conversations. Heavens! What would they think if the woman with the missing daughter smiled at something or dared to laugh at a joke?

She had heard from so many who stood in judgement saying things like, "You should have known better than to get involved with an Iranian," and, "What were you thinking letting your daughter go to Iran with her father? Don't you know what's going on over there?"

What she really needed from people was for them to ask her about her child. To ask her what Mari was like, what were her hobbies and how was Mari doing. She craved conversations about her daughter, but no one ever asked. People didn't know what to say and it created awkward social interactions.

Jodi's "happy thoughts" included cuddling with Mari while watching reruns of "The Golden Girls" and "I Love Lucy." Mari loved Lucy as much as Jodi had growing up. The happy memories helped Jodi escape the thoughts she perceived others had of the situation. The hours passed slowly as the plane droned along and Jodi's mind wandered from one thing to another. Time forced her to sit, but it didn't keep her mind from going from one subject to another and while crossing the Atlantic her thoughts went to her childhood and her mother. Her mother had laughingly called her the "demon child" the cause of her gray hair and wrinkles.

"I was the one that made her want to pull her hair out because of my thoughts and actions," said Jodi. She was the family's chief mischief maker and the creator of practical jokes designed to torment her brothers. She was the child who climbed too high in the maple trees in her yard. The one who had the first stitches and the one whose favorite thing to do was roll across the back yard on a rusty old barrel.

"I loved my old 55-gallon rusty barrel that I rolled with my bare feet across our back yard for hours, pretending I was a famous circus acrobat," Jodi said. She could still hear her mom's voice in her head. "Get some shoes on or you're going to get tetanus!"

Despite her mother's warning, Jodi would just keep rolling. Spring could never come fast enough when Jodi was young, so she could get the barrel out.

Jodi started thinking of her grandparents and the happy times with them. One memory that stood out was when Grandma Reed gave her a package of little brown paper lunch bags at the start of summer. Jodi thought it odd at first, because school had just finished, but her grandmother had an explanation. Jodi's mom had told her that Matt and Jodi played outside all summer long and that she had to repeatedly beg them to come inside at lunch time. With the brown sacks, they could take lunch with them and have a picnic every day. Jodi was thrilled!

"I would pack lunches for Matt and me and we would eat in our forts or eat in our camper. Sometimes their brother Vern would join them and we would sit by the little creek and plot our future, or sit on my barrel and fix world problems," Jodi recalled.

Remembering the fun she had with those lunch bags, had her thinking about paper bags, of all things. She thought about the number of paper bags she would buy for Mari, so they could have picnics together and plan the future.

Soon the "what if's" entered her mind and took over her thoughts.

"What if they won't release Mari to me? Well, then I would have to run with her into Greece where I know they will help us," Jodi would think. She had memorized what route she would take in the event that would happen.

"What if Mari doesn't recognize me?" She told herself that she would need to keep praying so that wouldn't happen.

"What if the plane crashes into the ocean?" Jodi reminded herself that Matt would bring Mari home and love her as his own.

"What if Kevin hurts me when he sees me?" She told herself that she would not let that be a possibility by staying one step ahead of him.

The what if's and thoughts of her childhood continued for hours, with emotion and logic playing verbal volleyball in Jodi's mind.

Jodi's thoughts were interrupted with an announcement from the captain that the plane was flying over Reykjavik, the capitol of Iceland.

Alarmed, Jodi thought that the plane had made a wrong turn. She reached to the seat in front of her to turn on the screen with the interactive map and then understood.

She followed an animation of the plane's journey over the Atlantic Ocean. The absurdity of her situation, flying on a plane to Istanbul via Iceland somehow cracked her up as she visualized herself in an updated version of "I Love Lucy". She couldn't stop laughing at herself. She really thought that sleep deprivation had set in.

She looked at the map again.

"Who does this? I'm over Iceland," she said aloud to no one. The unidentified man raised his eyes, but not his head as she continued her giggling and shaking her head in disbelief.

Her thoughts returned to the happy little town of her childhood. As she reflected back, she believes the memories that were returning to her was God's way of letting her know that she would be able to provide Mari with a wonderful childhood and the memories of the past two years and three months would melt away with time.

CHAPTER 20

MONDAY, AUG. 8, 2011
ATATURK AIRPORT; ISTANBUL TURKEY
(BRAND NEW WORLD)

JODI FELT THE PLANE BEGIN its descent and looked out the window down on Istanbul. The port city looked so tranquil from above, with sandy beaches disappearing into a shimmering blue sea. She could see several multi-storied buildings and from above, the city looking modern with its wide highways and green spaces. She could also see its beautiful mosques, when the plane was turning to approach the runway. She knew then that she really had made it!

Knowing her phone would not work in Turkey frightened Jodi. She was finally in Istanbul, Turkey a city with a population of approximately 14 million and only knew two people. One was in an orphanage, most likely unable to comprehend what happened to her world and the other was on the loose in the city, probably planning her demise.

As she prepared to get off of the plane, she wondered about the FBI legat that was meeting her and if he knew where Mari was being held. Did he know the whereabouts of Kevin? It made her skin crawl to think that Kevin could be watching for her and she wouldn't know it; it was an intense, scary feeling.

At the time she was having those feelings, her emotional side took over. She couldn't believe she was actually in the same country as her daughter. She couldn't wait to see her, so she could hug her, love her and take her home. She felt her stomach leap, like the first rush after climbing a hill on a roller coaster and anticipating the ride down.

She knew that the FBI Legal Attaché (Legat) in Istanbul would be meeting her at a kiosk. Robby had been in touch with him throughout the ordeal, and even though Jodi had not met him, she trusted Robby's judgement and knowledge of the legat. Because of the mistake being made with Mari being returned to her father only 24 hours before, Jodi's trust in the Turkish system or anyone else didn't exist anymore.

She questioned Robby over and over again about how she would know Mike, the legat. How would she know he was really who he was supposed to be. Robby told Mike his middle name and Jodi was told to confirm his identity by asking him that name. She felt comfortable with that plan.

As people began moving forward to exit the plane, Jodi waited, having been seated in the back. She prayed to God to give her strength and courage. It was the first time she had bargained with God, asking Him if He would help her get Mari home and keep her safe; she would forever spend her days on earth helping other families locate their missing loved ones. She finished her prayers and felt unseen hands on her shoulders, guiding her as she walked off the plane and into Istanbul.

Donna had directed Jodi on what to say when she reached customs and passport control. She was to tell them where she was staying and that she was in Turkey on a vacation. Under no circumstances was she to tell them why she was really there. She nervously approached the passport booth.

"Passport!" demanded an unsmiling man.

Jodi felt like she was going to have a humiliating anxiety attack in public. Her hands were sweaty and she felt as if she couldn't breathe. What if they didn't let her in the country?

"Why are you in Istanbul?" The man asked while looking down at her passport.

"I am on vacation and staying at the Sheraton," Jodi responded quickly.

"You are traveling alone?" The man looked at Jodi oddly as he questioned her. He began entering her information into a computer.

"Yes. I have friends here," Jodi said, as coached by Donna.

The man looked up at Jodi, gazing at her for a few seconds.

"Please go ahead and good luck to you."

Jodi was relieved. She was allowed to enter Istanbul and would be able to get to her daughter.

She walked out into the terminal, a brightly lit modern corridor filled with hundreds of people. She recognized dozens of retail stores offering all sorts of food, drink and clothing. Jodi was struck by how modern Istanbul appeared - a judgment that she would quickly be changing.

She walked swiftly because she still had to retrieve a small suitcase from baggage claim. She found the corresponding carousel and had a few minutes to just look around.

It was overwhelming to think about where she was standing; being only miles away from Mari, instead of halfway around the world. She felt a surge of love for her daughter, wanting to provide her with the best life possible and found herself tearing up at the thought. She passed it off as exhaustion, mixed with anxiety. Thoughts of how much she loved that little beauty overwhelmed her and she felt very alone.

She began to focus on her surroundings, a distraction to help control her emotions. It was a beautiful airport and very modern. She hadn't been sure what to expect, because she hadn't had time to think about it. Not one ethnic group of people stood out, appearing to her as a melting pot of travelers. Was anyone else there to do what she was about to do? She didn't think so.

The carousel began moving and her attention was focused on searching for her suitcase. She spotted it, bent over to reach it and put it on the floor, while extending the handle. She walked with it to where she thought the FBI legat would be. Her eyes were constantly scanning the mass of people, because the thought of Kevin being able to see her was terrifying. She saw someone she thought must be the FBI legat in the distance. She walked closer, not quite certain and then the man smiled directly at her.

She knew it was him as he approached her. He took her suitcase and introduced himself.

"I recognized you from Robby's description, Jodi," Mike said.

She was relieved and began walking with him.

"Aren't you going to ask me Robby's middle name?" he questioned with a smile.

At the time, Jodi felt a little foolish for doubting it would be Mike and for having Robby set up the question to confirm his identify. She chuckled as she said, "It's OK, and I'm good."

Mike told her Robby's middle name for good measure and Jodi felt even more at ease.

Mike's vehicle was parked outside of the terminal. As they approached it, he said he had been working with Robby and Donna and that they thought very highly of Jodi. Instead of small talk, Mike began telling Jodi about work that still needed to be accomplished. First they would go to the American consulate in the city for a briefing with the State Department.

She recalled her right-brained-self asking, "Who does this?" Her left brain answering, "People, who want to get their children home, do this."

"Let me get that door for you Jodi, it's very heavy," Mike offered. The Land Rover he was driving was fascinating to say the least. He went on to tell her that the doors were hard to open because of their weight. They were bullet proof to keep passengers secure.

Jodi was trying to focus on what Mike was telling her, but couldn't. As Mike drove through the city, he was basically serving as a tour guide, providing Jodi with what, under normal circumstances, would be fascinating facts about the cosmopolitan city.

Where are you Kevin? What are you doing?

Mike explained that the famous mall in Istanbul was within walking distance of the Sheraton she would be staying in. The water at the hotel was fine to drink. In fact, most of the city water was safe to drink, according to Mike. He gave her a weather update, saying the temperature should be quite warm that week.

"The restaurants are great, too," Mike continued, but all Jodi heard was, "blah, blah, blah, blah, blah."

"I'm here to get my daughter and get the hell out of here," Jodi said briskly and sounding rather gruff.

Her comment kind of stopped Mike in his tracks, but he quickly and very nicely said, " I understand why you are here, but sometimes it takes a while to go through all of the paper work and court procedures to get a child out from Turkish custody. You may be here for a long time," He repeated what Jodi had been told several times while still in the states.

Jodi appreciated his kind words, but at the time she was thinking about the things she had studied about the country. Things like Turkish men and women and how they interact with Westerners. She had also studied the language, its culture and the layout of the city. She could recall where mosques were located and other landmarks, which would guide her through the city. Above all, she had learned that American money was king in the country.

The hell I will!

Her thought was unspoken as she told Mike she didn't expect to be in the country for long.

He reminded Jodi that the FBI and the State Department could do very little for her while she complied with the actual procedures that were expected of her. Agency staff would be there for her and she would have access to them for things she might need, but it was up to her to work with the attorney she had hired.

Before she traveled to Turkey, she was informed that her Turkish attorney would be on vacation on a private yacht in the middle of the

Mediterranean Sea. In his absence, he assigned interns who would walk her through the procedures until he returned.

Mike noted that because the plane had been delayed in New York, there was no time to check in to the hotel. They had to get to a briefing at the consulate and then back to the hotel where Jodi's Turkish attorneys would be meeting her. The attorneys would be escorting her to the prosecutor's office that very afternoon.

As they were driving through the city Jodi was pleased that she recognized things she had studied and memorized from pictures; mosques, statues, the CNN building! She also knew the road they were on, so she knew how to get to the American consulate. She spotted it before Mike pointed it out, which added to her confidence. She finally felt grounded and that she had control of her situation.

"I felt powerful and strong and I truly didn't want to hear how great Istanbul was." Jodi said.

Jodi thought Mike was a good guy. He had told her his son was visiting and had arrived a few days earlier and that he would be staying with his father for a while. Mike looked the part of an FBI agent, like an actor who had been cast in the role. He was a bald and buff good-looking man, who had an air of seriousness about him, which made her think that no one would want to be on his bad side.

Mike continued to talk as they pulled up to the consulate. Guards came out of the building and walked around the entire vehicle. One of the guards used a mirror attached to the end of a stick to search the vehicle's exterior, as well – from top to bottom and underneath.

Mike sensing Jodi's curiosity and nerves, explained.

"Anytime a vehicle goes out of the complex and returns to the consulate, it is checked for bombs," he said smoothly.

You can do this; don't be scared, God is with you.

Mike and Jodi walked from the parking lot and into the building. They were buzzed in and entered into a secured area. Jodi viewed guards behind glass, which she assumed was bullet proof, and was asked to turn over her passport and any cell phones and computers she may have with her. She complied with the request and was surprised when Mike was asked to do the same.

She followed Mike through security and into the interior of the consulate. It was very beautiful, bright and airy. Artwork tastefully hung on its high walls, creating a peaceful atmosphere. After her observations, the reality of where she was hit her and she began feeling slightly panicked.

I need to get to Mari!

Nothing was moving fast enough for her. Jodi described feeling as if her skin was the only thing holding her together and everything inside of her was trying to get to her daughter. She needed to separate herself from Mike for a moment and asked if she could use a restroom.

"Of course," said Mike, "Right this way." He reminded Jodi of Robby by being so polite and nice to her.

Jodi walked into the restroom and just leaned against a wall to breathe. She told herself she had to get it together, that she didn't have time to fall apart. She washed her hands and looked at herself in the mirror. She almost didn't recognize herself. She looked so serious. The spark was gone from her eyes and she looked like exactly who she was - a scared mother who had no idea what would be coming next. "Get it together, Mari is counting on you!" she said, while pointing to her reflection in the mirror.

She felt better when she exited the restroom and rejoined Mike, who was waiting outside the door. They began walking.

"It's lunch time here and you need to eat Jodi," Mike calmly said. "Besides I'm treating!"

Jodi knew he meant it as a joke, but didn't smile back at him and just kept putting one foot in front of the other. She didn't have time to eat and didn't know if Mari was being fed. Food was the last thing on her mind.

"The ladies from the State Department will get their food and meet us in my office," Mike continued.

Jodi felt like screaming, trying to get him to understand she didn't have time for lunch, all she wanted to do was to reach Mari.

"OK, but can we hurry this along?" her impatience showing.

Mike glanced down at her, his smile fading. His expression told her he understood but that she had to meet with them and have papers signed, which was all part of the procedure.

As she approached the cafeteria, she saw a buffet which reminded her of her guilt about the situation. She was standing there, looking at a beautiful arrangement of food; European, Turkish and American. She could select whatever looked good to her and eat how much she wanted. She thought of Mari sitting in an orphanage, alone, wondering what would happen to her and if her mother would really be coming to get her. Jodi teared up and swallowed hard. Mike noticed and asked if she was alright.

Jodi nodded as she dished a small amount of rice, watermelon and tomatoes on her plate.

"Is that all you want?" Mike asked her.

Again, Jodi told him she didn't have time to eat, that what she needed was to get to Mari.

The people who worked at the consulate were kind to Jodi, but she could feel they knew she was the American mom coming to get her daughter. The looks in her direction lasted a little longer than Jodi was comfortable with.

In Mike's office, they set their lunch trays down on a conference table. He told her the ladies would be arriving soon. He excused himself, telling Jodi he owed Robby a phone call to tell him that she had arrived. Jodi could hear his side of the conversation.

"I believe she's doing fine, but she's very anxious and determined. I will let you know," she heard Mike say. Jodi could not hear much else as he started talking quietly and was too far away. Besides, her mind was on Mari.

Two women entered the agent's office. They were professionally dressed and beautiful. One of them was blonde and obviously American.

Jodi thought the brunette might be of Turkish descent. They carried their lunches and casually sat down. In soft voices, they introduced themselves to Jodi. She realized that the blonde woman was Lisa, whom she had spoken with the night before and they had both been with Mari after she was separated from her father.

Both of the women appeared to be very relaxed, which bothered Jodi. In all of her communications with anyone who would listen, Jodi tried to get them to understand that, to the world, Mari was but one little girl, but to Jodi, "she was the world."

She told herself that they were relaxed to reassure her and keep her calm, but it wasn't working.

Lisa and her associate explained what papers needed signing, including an emergency passport document to get Mari out of Turkey, because her passport was missing. Kevin and Mari had been traveling to Turkey with falsified documents and aliases and it was believed that Mari was traveling under a false Iranian passport and that Kevin would not give up her American one.

Jodi had already signed her parental rights over to the Turkish government to act on Mari's behalf before she left for Turkey. Now, she had to sign another copy to replace the one she had faxed to them. She hated signing the document more than anything, but didn't have a choice as it was the only way to get Mari away from Kevin and for Mari to be safe from him, as well. She had to will her hand to put pen to paper.

"What do you want to know about Turkey?" Lisa asked her.

Jodi looked at her like she was insane. She looked at Lisa with arched eyebrows, looked at the other woman and then at Mike, who sensed the tension.

"I just want to know how Mari is! I want to go to my daughter!" Jodi stated losing her patience.

Without hesitation, Lisa began telling Jodi about the orphanage and its conditions.

It was the first time Jodi was told the name of where her daughter was being held. They said the conditions were good there, but Mari was understandably very upset. Her doctors had said she was physically fine, but emotionally, she was a mess. Her eyesight was off, but they didn't know if it was from being so upset and crying, or if her eyes had been damaged in Iran. Jodi was told that the orphanage facility was extremely secure, and guarded around the clock.

She was then informed that Turkish law superseded any rights Kevin or Jodi had as Mari's biological parents. Mari belonged to the country, which would make all decisions regarding her wellbeing. Jodi also learned that the female general at the orphanage would be the one who decided who could see Mari. At this point, Jodi was told that both parents had a right to visit their daughter.

Jodi quickly told them of her concerns and of Kevin's threats towards Mari since she had been in Iran with him. She knew her voice sounded like she was begging them to believe her words.

"I needed them to understand that he would actually harm her, if given the chance, and that I needed their help in keeping him away from her," Jodi said.

They told her that both Robby and Donna, along with everyone else involved, were aware of Kevin's threats and that they were taking his warnings very seriously. Mike said he had witnessed Kevin's erratic behavior at the police station earlier that week and so he was also concerned about Kevin being anywhere near Mari or Jodi. Lisa and the other State Department employee said that they would convey all of the concerns to make certain that Turkish officials were aware of what had happened. However, it would be up to the general to make the final decision.

Jodi was wondering how much longer before the meeting would end, when Mike finally announced they needed to get Jodi to her hotel where her attorneys planned to meet her.

They said their goodbyes and were on the way to the hotel.

CHAPTER 21

Monday, Aug. 8, 2011 - 1 p.m.
Sheraton Maslak Istanbul Hotel
(First Impressions)

Jodi couldn't wait to get out of the consulate. She knew the meeting was important, but she was so close to seeing Mari, that she could feel the beat of every second that day. The overwhelming feeling of being so close to Mari and not being in control of when she could go to her was frustrating, as was having to rein in her instinct to race to her daughter.

Mike drove her to the hotel and explained that he lived around the corner, so if she needed anything, to just call and he would be there. He kindly said that if she became scared, or needed someone to talk with or walk with, she could call on him.

She believed he knew her thoughts were somewhere else as he repeated his words twice. She appreciated his kind words but the need to get to Mari was so much greater then listening or even comprehending what he said.

When they arrived at the hotel, Jodi knew Mike would be a gentleman and help her with her luggage as he walked her in. He was that kind. Unfortunately, she had learned over the past 800 days that no one quite moved fast enough for her and to try and be patient. She had learned to take a deep breath and just let people move at their pace.

However, Mike moved quickly, knowing that Jodi's anxiety level was most likely over the top. Jodi thought it was quite interesting to watch him analyzing her. Having been around the FBI for a long time she recognized the type of observation. She imagined that Mike thought she was crazy because of her actions and the fact that she believed she would only be in Turkey a short time.

She understood that once she was dropped off at the hotel, the job of getting Mari released from the orphanage was solely on her and deep inside she knew what it would take to achieve it.

"Maneuvering around the city, avoiding Kevin and begging Turkish authorities to help me was on my shoulders. I am sure they thought me crazy to believe I could do it," Jodi later said.

Donna had secured her flight to and from Istanbul; a round trip ticket for Jodi and a one-way flight for Mari. Donna said she had to give the airline a return date, so she provided a return date of Aug. 18. Donna had told her not to worry, because the end date could be changed to extend the stay and that they could worry about that as it got closer.

Jodi said it never had entered her mind that she would be there until the 18th and also couldn't fathom being there any longer, even though she had been told that the process of getting a child out of Turkish custody would take time. It was a delicate process and usually took weeks, months and sometimes years. She said she never let herself think that was even possible. She continuously prayed and visualized Mari home, to avoid the thought.

She wondered briefly if Kevin was watching her, as she arrived at the hotel.

"Was he out there just waiting to confront me or worse?"

As Jodi was questioning Kevin's whereabouts, she recalled an email she had received on Saturday from Robby; a message to him from the FBI legate in Turkey:

Saturday, August 6, 2011 8:30 a.m.

"When she gets to the airport, she will get off the plane and follow all the other tourists to immigration. Before getting in the immigration line, she

needs to buy a tourist visa at the visa window for 20 dollars. Then go through immigration and get her baggage. She then leaves the baggage area into the main airport. She should go right to the Vodaphone kiosk which is where I will be.

"I will be at the airport to meet her. She should be ready to meet with her lawyer Monday afternoon or Tuesday morning. Kevin will not know where she is staying unless she tells someone. Only her lawyer needs to know where she will be."

Jodi had learned to tell very little about herself to other people over the past 800 days, so not telling anyone where she was staying in Istanbul was very easy for her. She had shown Matt and Nancy the hotel confirmation that Donna had sent and Nancy had written all of the information down.

"Everyone involved knew the danger level and the importance of keeping the business of getting Mari home to ourselves."

When they entered the hotel, Jodi saw that it was a very beautiful place. It was so overwhelmingly large, that it took her breath away. Marble floors lined by marble walls made the lobby look like a scene out of a movie. A jewelry store caught her eye as there were many "Nazur Boncurgu" hanging, displayed in its windows. She found the jewelry piece very interesting and knew if circumstances were different, she would have made time to explore the store.

The ladies from the embassy had brought little gifts for Mari and Jodi and had given Jodi a key chain with a Nazar Boncurgu on it. They told her it was custom to give it to visitors new to Turkey and that the amulet would bring her good luck and keep her safe against an evil eye. She learned from them that the making of the Nazar Boncugu is a master trade that stretches back more than 3,000 years. It is one of Turkey's most purchased souvenir and good luck charm. The glass bead is characterized by a sea blue glass field with a blue or black dot superimposed on a white or yellow center.

The lobby décor was a perfect blend of European, Middle Eastern and American décor – it was posh and gorgeous.

Mike handled the details of checking her in. Jodi was memorizing her surroundings when the man at the reception desk asked her for a credit card to secure her room. She noticed he spoke very good English which gave her a sense of calm, knowing someone who spoke English in case she needed it.

She handed him the credit card and chuckled to herself knowing there couldn't have been more than $50 left on its limit. Jodi had spent everything she had to get to this point and she knew she had enough cash to get done what she came to do.

As the young man at reception handed her card back, he asked for her signature. She looked over at Mike and smiled. It was the first time she had really looked at him.

"What was it about these FBI agents I had met? Were they all that kind and nice, or was I just extremely blessed?"

It seemed funny to Jodi that she noticed certain traits in FBI agents she'd known the past couple of years. Individual agents she met all carried themselves with a sense of pride. Confidence "oozed out their pores" and it was comforting to her that the FBI was the agency on the front line helping her. She kept making mental notes to thank them all when their work was done and forever praise them.

Before Mike left, he reminded Jodi that her attorneys were on their way and that they would arrive shortly.

"Jodi, you are safe here. Do what you came to do. I will be in contact with you throughout this and in contact with Robby. Call me if you need anything." Mike said, as if anticipating her anxiety.

Do what you came to do.

She didn't watch Mike leave, but jogged to the elevator with her bags and brief case. With key in hand, she got on the elevator, accompanied by several suited men. They looked to be from other countries and kept looking at Jodi, as if studying her.

Come on 14th floor!

Jodi imagined she looked a little out of sorts and probably a little disheveled. She had been about seven days without getting much sleep and she had just traveled half way around the world.

"Are you here on vacation?" The tall man to her left asked. She wasn't certain he was talking to her, but when she lifted her head; she saw he was looking directly at her. She felt trapped. Being trapped in an elevator with strange people was high on Jodi's list of stressful situations, so her humorous side took over as it always had.

"Well, yes I guess you could call it that." She said, laughing. Jodi knew she wasn't laughing out of humor, but anxiety.

"Are you by yourself?" he asked.

Oh, Lord, is this man going to hit on me?

At this point the other three men looked over at her. She stood up straighter and looked directly at him.

"No, I am traveling with the FBI on business."

She hoped that was enough information to make him stop talking to her and to stop the others from watching them. She hoped that he knew what the FBI was. Jodi felt she was in panic mode and needed to get to her room, so she could hear from her Turkish attorneys.

It worked! The man just nodded and smiled and didn't ask anything else. The other men in the elevator turned around and Jodi viewed the elevator lights marking the floors; 12, 13 and then 14! When the doors opened, she pushed past the men quickly and hurried to her room.

She unlocked the door and walked into the room, pulling her suitcase behind her, staring at what she saw. The corner room with windows wrapping around three-quarters of it provided a stunning view of Istanbul. Jodi walked up to the windows and placed her hands on the smooth glass allowing her eyes to scan the panoramic view of Istanbul.

This isn't what I studied. This isn't the map of Istanbul I know.

She suddenly felt alone and she let her eyes roam over the city, which seemed to go on for miles and miles. She could not see an end in any direction. In a city of more than 14 million people, Mari and Jodi only knew each other, and at this point, she still didn't know the address where Mari was being held.

Jodi told herself to remember what she had studied and that Mari was depending on her; that she promised her daughter she would be coming for her. As if God could hear her thoughts and feel her pain, she noticed a mosque she had studied and its location in proximity to the hotel. She slowly began recognizing even more landmarks. Her body responded to her brain and the more she focused on the landscape, the calmer she became.

Within minutes the hotel room phone rang.

"Hello Jodi, this is Elif. I am your attorney. Are you ready? We need to get to the prosecutor's office."

Elif's English was very good and Jodi remembered at the time thinking she sounded very young.

"Yes, I will be right down."

When she entered the lobby, she was approached by a young man and Elif. The attractive young man and woman appeared to be in their late 20's and seemed very excited to meet her. They exchanged introductions as they shook hands and Elif handed Jodi yet another Nazar Boncugu.

"This is to keep you safe in the city," Elif said.

The blue eye amulet from Elif was on a braided black rope which could be worn as a necklace. So not to insult their beautiful gift to her, Jodi set her bags down and placed the charm over her head and around her neck. Both the man and Elif smiled. The young man introduced himself as Varol. He motioned that they needed to get moving and that they could talk in the cab.

They walked out of the hotel doors and again, Jodi sensed Kevin's eyes on her and the danger he represented. She looked down at her new good luck piece and smiled thinking of how she would have to learn more about the little magic piece she had been given twice within the last several hours.

CHAPTER 22

MONDAY, AUG. 8, 2011
PROSECUTOR'S OFFICE; ISTANBUL, TURKEY
(THREATS)

JODI WASN'T CERTAIN IF HER fear had exaggerated her senses, or if her faith was so strong that she knew without any doubt that God was guiding her, but she had become extra aware of her surroundings at all times and tried to physically position herself so that she would not be trapped.

She entered the cab first and scooted to the far side against the door, in case she needed to bolt out of the vehicle. Varol and Elif appeared to be nice, but in reality, Jodi did not know if they really were. They didn't work for the United States government, the FBI or the State Department, so she remained cautious of them.

The attorneys seemed very interested in Jodi's case and were posing many, many questions to her about herself and Mari. How she was doing? Did she really travel here all alone? They had heard how Mari's father had acted at the police station and wondered how Jodi felt about him. Varol and Elif conversed with her in English most of the time and once in a while, they would exchange words in Turkish. Jodi, again, was grateful she had taken the time to study their language and could understood most of what they were saying; however, she pretended not to understand. It was hard for her to keep from smiling at their thoughts.

For example, Elif said to Varol, "Jodi çok güzel. O Amerikalı görünmüyor. Neden abd hükümeti onu burada yalnız yolculuk izin verir? Ben o kızları babası ona, hastalarda ne olduğunu bilmediğini düşünüyorum."

What Jodi translated was that Elif said Jodi is very pretty and does not look American.

"Why would the United States government let her travel here alone? I think she doesn't know what her daughter's father is threatening to do to her."

Jodi said she thought Elif noticed her smiling when she said, "She doesn't look American."

"Do you understand Turkish, Jodi?" Elif prodded excitedly.

Jodi caught her error and quickly and politely answered, "No," and smiled. She had learned through her studies it was better to keep the secret to herself and just play ignorant when it came to the Turkish language.

Jodi wondered for a brief moment, just how does an American look American? Maybe Elif thought that all Americans looked like movie stars.

The more Jodi studied the lawyers, the more she thought how much they looked alike. Both were very attractive people, with dark brown hair and dark brown eyes. Elif's skin was a lighter tone and she reminded Jodi of Jennifer Lopez. Varol was tall and more reserved then Elif, and he was very interested in the details of her case. His questions when answered would provide him with more facts about what had happened, while Elif's questions were more personal.

Jodi knew that in an ordinary time in her life, she would have found the two of them fascinating and that they probably would have become friends. She could tell right away that their energy level matched hers and was grateful that she was beginning to feel comfortable around them. They appeared to know what they were doing and she was happy to have them representing her. Jodi knew that their boss was on vacation and she was OK with that at the time. She liked both of them.

They talked for several minutes about what Jodi believed would happen if Kevin and she had to confront each other. She conveyed her strong feelings that it would not be a good situation and they informed her that they had been told about Kevin's threats toward Jodi while he was at the police station.

As they continued to talk, it was as if Jodi's mind was split into several pieces and all of the pieces were functioning simultaneously. She couldn't say if her thoughts were just flipping from one to another every time there was a pause on one thought, or if she had just compartmentalized everything she needed to think about.

One part of her brain was watching where they were going. Jodi was looking for landmarks and streets she had memorized, acknowledging them and remembering when she found them. Another part of her mind was on Mari. How was she doing? Would she recognize her? Would she want to come home with her mother? Were her eyes getting better? Then in the shadowy part of her brain was the part which wondered, always, where Kevin was.

They arrived at the prosecutor's office. She had been told that prosecutors in Istanbul were like judges in the United States. They had the authority to make decisions and that when decisions were made, judges would just sign off in agreement. She was told the meeting was required so they could identify who she was, how the situation had developed and why the rescue was taking place in their country. Jodi was told to present the custody papers detailing her physical rights to Mari. Then, the prosecutor would set the next court date and declare when Jodi could visit Mari at the orphanage.

Looking at the building when they arrived gave Jodi a jolt, realizing again that she wasn't in America anymore. The building was very old and located on a very narrow street. It was several stories high and not very wide. It reminded her of an old bank building from the 1940s or 50s.

She began feeling more anxious as the three of them exited the cab and started toward the building.

Jodi's lawyers were on each side of Jodi, who was walking at a brisk pace. They walked up to a guard and stated their reason for being there. The guard did not speak as he nodded them through. He reminded Jodi of a guard she had seen outside of court houses in the U.S.; wearing a uniform and carrying a side arm and not speaking more than necessary.

Almost at that very instant they all heard someone screaming. Not an ear piercing scream Jodi had heard in the movies, but a deep bellowing at the top of one's lungs. Jodi's heart started thumping fast when she recognized who it was coming from.

All that stood between Jodi and Kevin was a single wall. She stopped in her tracks. Her lawyers, sensing the change in her, asked her what was wrong.

"That is Kevin... he is talking in Farsi. He is screaming that this is unfair and Mari should be released to him now." Jodi answered.

Kevin continued to scream in Farsi, saying he wanted to confront Jodi in person and that the United States did not have any say in what he wanted. She couldn't see who he was talking with because the door to the office was closed. It had been such a long time since Jodi had seen the man who was keeping her daughter from her.

I was scared beyond scared.

Varol looked at Elif, who took Jodi by the arm.

"Come on, we need to hide you."

They ran around a corner where they discovered a stairway and started running up to the next floor and continued running higher and higher. Jodi felt she didn't breathe the entire time and wasn't even winded. She was so frightened that Kevin would kill her and she would be unable to help Mari that it left her with an eerie calm, an automatic response which kicked in.

When they could go no higher, Varol located a side room. It was like a janitor's room with machinery systems, brooms and cleaning supplies. It was very noisy inside the room with some sort of system running, which Jodi guessed to be the air conditioning unit for the building. The room was about 7- feet-wide by 30-feet-long and it was very, very hot. There were two chairs sitting against the wall behind the fan unit and Varol told Jodi to sit down as he and Elif discussed what they should do next. Jodi listened in on their conversation as they conferred in Turkish, but was pretending to look out the back door which opened up to a balcony.

A worker came in through the door and questioned why they were there. Varol took control and told him that they needed a place to hide for a little while, explaining there was a man downstairs wanting to hurt the woman who they were working with.

"She is an American woman coming to rescue her daughter out of Iran," said Varol.

Jodi continued to look at this man and into his eyes. He was an older Turkish man, around 60, with graying hair around his ears and a bald spot on top of his head. He had a very kind face and kept looking at Jodi in the eye. He told Varol they could stay there as long as needed and he would make sure no one else would go into the little room. He said he would alert them if someone was on their way up who didn't look like he belonged. Jodi smiled at the man and nodded. He nodded in return and then left the very noisy and hot room.

Elif looked at Jodi and asked her again if she spoke Turkish. Jodi shook her head and her lawyers repeated, in English what they didn't know she had already heard. Elif was going to go downstairs and make it appear that her client was not with her. She would say that she was representing Jodi and had come to the prosecutor's office to learn what was happening.

Varol would stay upstairs with Jodi, in case Kevin got near her. Varol was a tall, strong man, but Jodi worried just as much about him and Elif at the time, as she did about herself and Mari.

Elif went downstairs to start proceedings with the prosecutor. She put her hand on Jodi's shoulder before she left and said, "No worry Jodi, we will get you through this."

Varol and Jodi lowered themselves to the chairs. She had two bottles of water in her bag and offered one to Varol, which he gratefully accepted. It was so hot in the room that they both started to sweat, but there was nowhere else for them to go. A light breeze was coming in through an open screened door at the end of the tunneled room, which helped very little.

The air conditioner was so loud that it was hard to hear Varol talk, unless the two of them leaned close to each other and almost shouted, but they were trying to be quiet. Varol looked at Jodi's bandaged hand and asked her what had happened. Jodi hesitated for a moment because she had forgotten about it. She told him the truth about when Mari had been released back into her father's custody and of how she had punched a wall again and again. Of course the emotion behind the act had subsided by that time and Jodi felt rather foolish telling him about what she had done to injure herself. To her great surprise, Varol told her he had heard about the botched rescue attempt two days before.

"It will be fine, it doesn't hurt," Jodi said, trying to prevent him from being uncomfortable. Her more immediate concern was how much she was sweating and how faint she felt from the heat. "I remember thinking this would be the best "Secret" underarm deodorant commercial ever," Jodi said, as the funny thought briefly crossed her mind.

She was grateful to God for her sense of humor. It brought her through the scariest points of her life. If anyone knew the funny thoughts she was thinking now, they most likely would think she had lost her mind.

Varol and Jodi continued talking. He told her he was fascinated that she had traveled all the way to Turkey alone with no one from the United States government helping her. She tried explaining to him the "whys" several times and in several ways, but he couldn't understand and said it was unimaginable.

"No woman should have to do this alone," he repeated and then slowly shook his head back and forth.

Jodi shrugged her shoulders and told him the line she had been saying for more than two years.

"To the world she may be only one little girl, but to me... she is the world."

Varol nodded and said he understood.

"You don't seem to be afraid?" Varol posed his observation as a question.

Jodi softly told him she was not, but was sure he could see fear in her eyes. She kept looking at her watch ... 30 minutes had passed, then 40 minutes and then 90. She thought she would go out of her mind. She couldn't fathom what was taking so long and told Varol that they needed to go check on things.

As Jodi was voicing her impatience, Elif called Varol. He put her on speaker, so Jodi could hear. Elif said she would be calling again in a few minutes to explain everything. She said that she was going to walk out of the building and that Varol and Jodi needed to get to children's police headquarters.

She said Kevin had lawyered up and had an attorney from the Iranian embassy with him. She told them she was walking to get a cab and was certain that they would be following her, because Kevin had demanded to know where Jodi was. Elif said she would lead Kevin and his lawyer far away from the children's police building and then would catch up with them there.

Jodi and Varol could hear Elif get into a cab and close the door. She told the cab driver to wait "just a second." And then heard her say, "There they are," when she told the cab driver to pull away slowly, so they could be followed.

She stayed on the phone for the next few minutes and said she could see them following her cab and for Jodi and Varol to get out of prosecutor's building and to the children's police facility.

As she rode in the taxi, Elif explained for the next few minutes about what had happened in the proceeding. Before the prosecutor could even ask her where Jodi was, Kevin began screaming and demanding to know Jodi's location. Elif said she told the prosecutor that Jodi was in the country, but because of the threats from Kevin and his actions, they were going to keep Jodi separated from him.

Kevin's Iranian attorney told Kevin to calm down and allow him to talk on his behalf. Elif said Kevin never took his eyes off of her and he looked angry and ready to pounce. Kevin's attorney went on to explain that his client had never intended to keep Mari in Iran and that he was a good father. He was upset because his rights as a father had been violated when the authorities separated him from his daughter. Elif said the prosecutor kept watching Kevin and his actions.

It was Elif's turn to explain the situation from Jodi's side.

"I have documents to prove that Mari's mother, Jodi Reed Homaune, has full custody of her daughter and that this man has kept her away from her daughter for more than two years and three months. He has made demands that in order for Jodi Reed Homaune to even talk to her daughter in Iran, she must pay him large amounts of money," Elif said.

She told them that Kevin interrupted her turn to talk four times and each time, the Iranian attorney tried to get Kevin to be quiet. Elif repeated how the prosecutor never took his eyes off of Kevin.

The prosecutor stamped the documents needed to release Mari from the orphanage to her mother. The next step in the process, said Elif, was that the prosecutor instructed Jodi and her attorneys to go to Children's Police Headquarters and obtain an escort to the orphanage and back. Elif said she believed the prosecutor thought his decision would calm Kevin down and make him think twice about his actions, but it had the opposite effect.

Kevin started shouting at Elif.

"You tell me where Jodi is, I demand to see her!"

Elif responded by telling him that it was none of his business any more.

"You tell her that I will find her, no matter how big this city is. You warn her!" Kevin screamed at the top of his lungs.

Elif said the prosecutor just watched him and dismissed everyone from his office. As Elif walked out of the office, she said she looked back and saw the prosecutor pick up his phone.

Varol hung up with Elif and promptly dialed his boss to report what was happening. They spoke very quickly and Jodi could make out just enough words to tell that he was relaying the phone call with Elif. The lead attorney told Varol to get Jodi out of the building safely, without anyone seeing her in case Kevin had people watching for her. He then asked to speak with Jodi to tell her things were going well, but not to get too excited, as they still had a long way to go.

Varol and Jodi went down the stairs, one floor at a time, with Varol looking around every corner to make sure the way was clear. At the bottom of the stairs, Jodi untied a scarf she had been wearing around her waist and placed it over her head. She put on her sunglasses. Again, her humor kept her steady, as what she was doing reminded her of a scene from "Scooby Doo," with people creeping around inside of buildings, anticipating a monster to sneak right up behind them.

CHAPTER 23

AUG. 8, 2011
TURKISH CHILDREN'S POLICE STATION
("MERHABA, NO TURKISH, ENGLISH!")

DURING THE CAB RIDE OVER to the children's police headquarters, Jodi started to realize again that time was not being her friend. Thoughts of Mari continued to crowd her mind. She had told her daughter that she was coming to see her and take her home but she had yet to talk with her since her arrival in Istanbul.

Then she realized how much she had accomplished in the five short hours since her arrival, besides being driven all over the city. Mike called as they were driving and said he had heard the prosecutor had signed the order. Jodi, hesitated, and then told him not to get too excited. Yes, the prosecutor had signed Mari's release, but now it was up to the children's police chief to follow the order. She told him she had talked with her lead attorney and that he told her there was still a lot to be done before Mari would be released to her mother's custody.

Mike told her to hang in there and that she was doing great and to call him if she needed anything. He said he would call Robby, and Jodi asked if he would also contact her brother to tell him she had landed and was doing OK. She begged Mike to call the orphanage to tell them of Kevin's new threats against her and to please, please not allow Kevin near Mari. Mike asked Jodi if she was really OK, and she told him again that she was fine. When she hung up with Mike, she leaned against the window of the cab to pray.

"Please keep Mari safe, Lord. Please send a message to her little heart so she knows that I'm here and I will see her soon. Please give me the strength to finish this and to give Mari the life she was born to have." As always, her prayers calmed her.

When the cab stopped moving, Jodi peered out to look at the building and was shocked by what she saw. Plain clothed men and woman surrounded the building and held machine guns against their chests. Her adrenaline started to run making her heart beat very fast. Jodi kept saying to herself, "God is with me every day. God is with me every day," which helped calm her nerves, again.

Her humor surfaced as it always did in tense situations and for a moment she imagined her brothers and her parents watching her get out of the cab and scanning her surroundings. In her mind, she could hear them saying, "Only you Jodi, only you," which made her inwardly chuckle for a second. The thought quickly passed as they walked towards the building and someone, whom she guessed to be a guard, approached them to ask their reason for being there.

Varol pulled out documents stating who they were and told him they had a meeting scheduled with the chief. The guard was wearing plain clothes and wore a badge on his chest. As Jodi's eyes wandered, observing, she noticed that all the men and women with machine guns were wearing the same identification badge.

It looked to her like the building had been taken over by those people, instead of them protecting what was inside. The women from the State Department had told Jodi that the Turkish government is very serious when it comes to its children. It considers every child in their custody theirs and takes every precaution to protect them. Jodi reminded herself that Mari was Turkey's child, for the moment.

The guard waved his machine gun towards the building to indicate that they could go forward. Another guard, a woman, came up beside them and never saying a word, followed them inside.

More guards walked inside with them as well, and Jodi observed that not one of them took their eyes off of her and that all of their fingers were positioned near the triggers of their guns. It dawned on her, that she was the odd person of the group, so she didn't smile or acknowledge their presence. She just kept walking. "Mommy Power" energy was coming over her and she knew she couldn't show she was intimidated. She needed to be strong for Mari, even though internally, she felt she was falling apart. She hoped that no one else could see that. She continued to firmly put one foot in front of the other, as she prepared herself emotionally to face the situation.

Once inside the building, the chief came out of his office to greet them and invited the group in. Visitors consisted of Varol, Jodi and two of his own guards. They entered the chief's office and Varol began explaining their reason for being there. The chief cut him off and said he was aware of the situation, because the prosecutor had called him and told him that he wanted a police escort for Jodi to take her wherever she needed to go.

Jodi sensed that the chief was not happy with the request. He started to explain that he would have to see the paperwork Elif was bringing before he proceeded. Jodi sensed that the police chief must not like the fact that the rescue was taking place in his city.

Four additional police agents came into the room and were asking their chief about details of other cases they were working on. They questioned who Jodi was. He said, "This is the American woman who is here to pick up her daughter."

They looked over and smiled at Jodi and continued to talk. She smiled back and became interested in what they were saying. The chief was telling them about her case. He was telling the officers he didn't know why it was being handled in Turkey.

"We have an Iranian sleeping on park benches, an American sleeping in a hotel and an American Iranian in an orphanage. None of them have any connection to our country, but yet here we are handling it." Laughing, he continued, "It is like the movie "Not Without My Daughter," only this is "Not Without My Daughter 2."'" They all started to laugh as Jodi checked her anger.

Varol looked at her, knowing then that she understood what they were saying. She didn't think they were mocking the situation, but were in awe that it was taking place in their country.

Jodi didn't take her eyes off of the police chief while she was sitting and waiting and could tell her intense gaze was making him feel uncomfortable. She thought she heard the chief question if she understood Turkish. He then asked Varol if she did and Varol looked at Jodi and said, "No, she doesn't." The police chief nodded, but continued his watch of the American woman.

Jodi asked Varol if she could use the restroom. Varol asked the chief, who instructed a female officer to escort Jodi to one of the building's public restrooms. The officer nodded her agreement and pointed for Jodi to come with her. Jodi followed her down a flight of stairs and into the restroom. The woman smiled at Jodi as she pointed to one of the several doors.

With broken English she said, "This is more modern for you."

Jodi wasn't quite certain what she meant and then the woman turned around and left. It felt good to have a moment alone. She finished her business and then took some time to look in the other doors. There were three. The others were facilities that she had heard about, but had never seen. Turkish facilities were basically a toilet on the floor where a person had to squat to use. A hose was situated close by to wash their bodies when they were done. Clean little towels and toilet tissue were located on the side. The "stalls" looked beautiful and had been constructed out of marble.

Jodi knew she had to get back quickly, but took a few moments as the restroom was so interesting to look at. On the counter where the sink was, she saw two spray bottles filled with what looked like water. They were pretty glass bottles topped with a spritzer. Jodi sprayed the contents from one bottle in the air and recognized the fragrance as rose water. Mari's Iranian grandmother had always sent her bottles of rose water to cook with and use as a skin fragrance. She had told her that when it was very hot in their country, they would use rose water to cool their skin. Jodi smiled at the bottles – it felt good to recognize something that belonged to their culture.

Feeling more comfortable after having a few minutes to regroup and breathe, Jodi exited and climbed the stairs. As she negotiated the final step, she felt a machine gun pressed against her stomach. It was held by a very large policeman who was screaming at her in Turkish. Jodi couldn't understand anything he was saying, because he was so angry and he kept pushing the weapon into her stomach. He was so loud, that people started to gather around. The officer continued to jab Jodi's stomach with the firearm.

Jodi stared at him as she said, "Merhaba, no Turkish, English!" and without thinking moved the machine gun's muzzle away from her stomach with her good hand holding on firmly to the barrel. She didn't take her eyes off of his.

I am not going down this way without Mari.

As Jodi was pushing the gun away, the police chief came out and yelled at the officer. All Jodi could understand was, "This is the American woman here to get her daughter!" The officer lowered his gun and nodded at Jodi to move on her way.

She followed the police chief back to where Varol was and saw that Elif had arrived. She asked her how she was doing and Elif said she was fine; that she had lost Kevin and his attorney, but they could talk about that at a later time.

The chief explained that the Iranian attorney had called the Turkish chief justice in Ankara (the capital of Turkey) and that the justice said he wanted to look into the prosecutor's decision. It wasn't reversed, just on hold, until he sorted out the mess. He said that he wanted no more mistakes made when it came to Mari.

Elif and Varol were upset and voiced their concerns about Kevin to the chief. He said he had witnessed Kevin's actions and the threats he had made. He had personally called the general at the orphanage and told her not to allow Kevin in to see Mari.

Jodi was vastly relieved to hear what he said about protecting Mari from Kevin, but watching the chief's actions convinced her that he was not on her side, or maybe no one's side. He just seemed to want to be finished with the entire situation.

Her phone rang and it was Mike again. "What is happening Jodi?" he said with a curious tone.

Everything is falling apart again, Mike." Jodi said, with panic in her voice. "They said that the prosecutor's decision is on hold, and to top it off, the Turkish chief justice is involved now and said he wants answers on what is happening."

Mike instructed Jodi to hang on while he investigated exactly what was going on.

Everything was unraveling again before Jodi's eyes. The attorneys said that she would have to return to the hotel, because their boss was flying in from the Mediterranean to take over. They told her that the State Department was once again involved and that someone from there would be calling her.

Jodi felt cheated. She had done all of the work required and now it was too late to see Mari because visitation hours had ended at the orphanage.

"What will Mari be thinking?" Jodi thought. "She doesn't even know I'm in the country yet."

She walked out of the police station in tears and into a cab with her attorneys. They continued to talk between themselves as she stared out of the window on the drive back to the hotel. She prayed to ask God to send Mari a message that she was very close to seeing her.

After she prayed she called Mike and begged him to get the women from the consulate to go to Mari and explain the situation and to have her daughter call her. She knew without a doubt that Mari needed to know her mother was there. She told Mike it would help in keeping herself sane. Mike listened and didn't say a word then told her he would handle it.

CHAPTER 24

Monday, Aug. 8, 2011 – 8 p.m.
Sheraton Maslak Istanbul Hotel
(Evening meeting with Turkish attorney)

After Jodi arrived at her hotel, she went directly to her room. She closed the door and crumbled, exhausted and feeling defeated at not being able to hurry things along.

"I was so close to Mari, but couldn't be with her," Jodi said.

Mari's absence and the tension of the last few days, had taken a toll. Physically and mentally, Jodi felt at the breaking point. Her heart ached with a fierce longing to see her daughter. A diary entry from Christmas Day summed up her feelings:

Dec. 25, 2010

> *I never thought it possible that a heart could break from loving someone so much. Loving someone so much means protecting them, loving every little thing about them; being the one person that they can count on. I promise you Mari, Mommy will figure out how to get you home.*

She looked out the window, her view overlooking twilight in the city. She gazed down on the hundreds of buildings casting long shadows in the early evening sun and wondered which one of them held her daughter.

Jodi knew that it was not possible to really know, but for those few moments, it was all she could do.

She heard her phone ringing, interrupting her search. It was a call from her lead attorney, Murat. He had called Jodi to say he was on his way to the airport after having had to cut his vacation short. People from the State Department had contacted him on his boat and told him that the process was becoming a real mess.

He said that Elif and Varol had also called him to give him an update about Kevin's actions and what had taken place with the chief justice.

"I have talked with the State Department and they will go to the American embassy in Ankara tomorrow morning and we will get an answer on why this is halted," Murat told Jodi.

He said that he would arrive at the hotel around 8 p.m. and then they could try to figure out what to do next.

Immediately after Jodi hung up with Murat, Mike called her and confirmed something had gone wrong. The decision was not reversed, but the chief justice wanted more details before he allowed the new custody arrangement to go through, confirming he did not want any more mistakes made, especially under his jurisdiction.

Mike told Jodi he would have answers for her in the morning. Before he hung up, he asked if she wanted him to come by her hotel, if she felt secure enough and what he could he do to help. She told him not to worry, but in reality, she admitted to herself, she was scared to death. Earlier during the day when she first met Mike, he had told her that he was having a small party for his son. Jodi didn't want to interrupt his party and told him that she needed time to think. She convinced Mike that she was OK by telling him that Murat was coming to the hotel that evening so they could talk.

Months before, Agent Donna had given Jodi some great advice about what to do when she felt overwhelmed and frustrated. She said it helped to get into a shower, turn it on full blast and scream at the top of her lungs.

Jodi decided to take a quick shower, as she was sure she must "smell" having just flown half way around the world. She hadn't slept in seven nights and wasn't sure if she had eaten anything. On top of that, she had waited in the top of a building for more than an hour where it was every bit of 110 degrees, with no air flow. Yes, she was sure she smelled, as she wrinkled her nose.

In the huge, modern bathroom, Jodi reached into the shower and figured out how to turn it on and dial it to the right temperature – steaming hot. She put Donna's advice into action and finally broke down. She may or may not have screamed but within moments of her emotional release, she felt a familiar feeling enter her consciousness replacing the helplessness she was feeling. "Mommy Power" returned and Jodi told herself, "I can do this. I have prepared for 800 days to get my daughter back." An intensive surge of energy filled her.

You can do this; don't let Kevin destroy you and Mari.

She dried herself off, looked in the mirror and saw confidence. She decided that no matter what her attorney said she needed to do, she was going to do it.

Murat arrived in the lobby and called Jodi.

"Do you have a date tonight?" he asked her, chuckling at his own joke.

Jodi wasn't sure how she should respond. She was experienced enough in her quest that she knew she must think very carefully before she answered him. Before she said anything, Murat quickly asked if she would mind going out to dinner with him. Had she already eaten? Jodi paused trying to remember the last time she had. She honestly didn't know, but didn't feel hungry.

"No, I haven't eaten anything and I'm hungry, so yes, let's go to dinner and talk," she said. Was he flirting with her? His tone sounded playful. She wondered if he was serious about helping her and what he was really expecting from her, alone and desperate to get Mari out of the orphanage and both of them out of the country.

Jodi rode the elevator down to the lobby. As the elevator doors opened, Jodi searched the room for the attorney while looking to see if Kevin was around. She knew hotel security was aware of her situation, but she knew her ex-husband better than anyone else did in Turkey. At this point, his daughter had been taken from him; he knew Jodi was in the country and that she had lied to him for two years. She knew he was trying to find her and that he was out for revenge.

Before stepping away from the bank of elevators, Jodi searched the lobby again. She didn't see anyone looking for her, so she strolled around the lobby. The staff was aware of who she was - the American woman who had come to rescue her child, who had been kidnapped by her Iranian father.

"Hello," was repeated several times as she walked past a number of hotel employees.

A man approached Jodi and held out his hand for her to shake, smiling. He said he recognized her from the pictures she had sent him.

"Glad to meet you," she heard Murat say.

Jodi's first impression of him was that he looked like a kind man. As they went outside, he stepped back to allow Jodi to go ahead of him. It was still very warm and the sun was still high. She noticed that he was wearing casual attire, having come straight from his yacht.

Her attorney stood at the curb and signaled for a cab which would take them to a mall area close to the hotel. On the way, he kept up a barrage of questions to Jodi. Was she OK? Did she trust him to take her to dinner and talk about the case? Did she travel to Turkey on her own? Was the FBI protecting her while she was there? Was the State Department providing her with any protection while she was in Istanbul?

"Yes, yes, yes, no and kind of," she answered. Why was he asking anyway? It made her feel a little unsettled and wary of his motives. She hoped it was just his natural curiosity.

They were seated at an outside bistro/restaurant and Murat asked Jodi if she wanted a beer or a Coke.

"No to both, water will be fine," she said.

"You are not like most Americans I have met," Murat observed. Jodi wasn't sure what that meant and frankly, she didn't care.

He asked her what she wanted to eat.

"It doesn't matter, would you mind ordering for both of us?" Jodi responded.

She could tell her response pleased him, yet something was telling her to be very careful around this man.

I wish so much that Elif and Varol were here.

He proceeded to ask her more questions, saying that he had never seen a case where both governments were so rattled and had their "higher ups" so involved.

"Why is this? Why were the red Interpol warnings taken off Kevin?" he questioned.

He said he did not understand why and Jodi told him neither did she, but they were and Kevin was a free man.

Once dinner arrived, Jodi realized how hungry she was and dove in. She wasn't sure what the look on his face meant as she ate.

"Why is he looking at me that way?" she thought. She didn't have to wonder for long.

"I am sitting here at dinner with this beautiful American woman, who has traveled half-way around the world to get her daughter. No one has come with her and there is no protection around her." Then he sounded angry as he said, "I can't believe the U.S. government has no protections for you! I could be a serial killer or just a bad man and yet here you are eating bread with me, trusting me to help get your daughter back."

Jodi calmly answered while looking Murat straight in the eye, "I am in Turkey for one reason, which is to take my daughter back to the United States."

She told him she had been promised that she would see Mari that day and that it did not happen because of time restraints at the orphanage and all of the time she had spent at the prosecutor's office.

"Either you can take me to see my daughter tomorrow, or I will take a cab and go on my own. I will take my chances of running into Kevin.

I'm not doing anything else until I see Mari and make sure that she is safe!" Jodi burst out. The look on Murat's face as he studied her during her tirade gave her an uneasy feeling.

"You are willing to do anything?" the attorney smiled slyly. Jodi wasn't sure what he meant, but didn't care. Wait a minute, she thought - anything? For Mari? Yes, anything, but she absolutely would not let him know that.

Murat then received a phone call and as he was speaking in Turkish to the other party, Jodi studied him, knowing that Turkish men appreciated others noticing details such as eye color, clothes, shoes and accessories. She figured he wasn't much older than she, a good looking man, who was physically fit. He had dark hair and light eyes. His personality was strong and Jodi believed that the man must not like to lose at anything.

As she was studying him, his facial expression changed and he started smiling at her, giving her the universal thumbs-up sign. She presumed he was hearing good news. After he put his phone down, Murat put his hand to his forehead.

"Never in all my days have I seen this!" he exclaimed.

"What?" Jodi questioned, leaning forward in her seat.

Murat told Jodi that he had just spoken with Kevin's Iranian lawyer, who had called to tell him that Kevin refused to pay him any money to represent him. He told Murat that he intended to dismiss himself from the case, because Kevin was a "piece of work."

The Iranian attorney said he had caught Kevin in several lies since they met and he told Murat to keep Jodi away from Kevin. He was positive that Kevin had traveled to Turkey to physical hurt her or worse. The attorney then emphatically said he wasn't going to be part of anything like that, and as a professional courtesy was informing Murat.

Murat told Jodi he had to think for a second and asked her to please be patient with him for a few more minutes.

"I know you have a million questions, but I have to think," Murat repeated.

Jodi wondered what else Murat had been told, but had to trust what he would tell. She could only hear part of the conversation and it was difficult for her to understand Turkish when it was spoken so quickly. She was trying very hard to understand the language and it frustrated her when she couldn't.

Jodi waited patiently for what felt like an hour, but was actually just a few minutes. Murat held his head with his hand and was being very dramatic about it.

When he finally broke his silence he told Jodi that she needed to get herself and her daughter out of the country as fast as possible. He told her the situation was not good and then told her what they needed to do in order to make it happen.

"We need signatures from another two judges to release the paper work to the police, and then the warden of the orphanage will release Mari over to you. This will also satisfy the Chief Justice. I am going to try to get Kevin to sign a piece of paper saying he wants you to take Mari to America. If he agrees to this without any problems, now or in the future, you can take her to America immediately. I am going to get his Iranian attorney to work for you, and act as an interpreter for us with Kevin. You are going to have to face Kevin and plead with him to do this, as well as I. This is going to cost you a lot of money while you are here.

Before Murat could call the Iranian attorney back, Kevin himself called Murat and told him that he did not want an attorney anymore. He said he did not like his attorney and he needed to see Jodi face-to-face to talk and finish this. Jodi instantly tensed, wondering how Kevin was able to call her attorney. Did he know where they were at that very moment? She tried to hide her anxiety as she scanned the restaurant looking for Kevin. (Jodi later learned that he had received Murat's number from his attorney at the prosecutor's office earlier that day.)

Murat questioned Kevin as to why he wanted to see Jodi. Kevin insisted that it was how it was going to be, or he would find another attorney to take the case. Murat asked Kevin again why that had to take place

- why not work together to get Mari out of the orphanage. Kevin said he had to see Jodi face-to-face and "that was that."

Jodi's attorney told Kevin that he would try and get the message to Jodi, to ask her what she wanted to do. He advised Kevin to keep his attorney, saying he thought him to be a good man and for him to call his attorney in one hour and talk with him. Kevin told him that he would.

Murat then dialed the Iranian attorney and asked him to keep representing Kevin and that Jodi was prepared to pay him to act as Kevin's attorney, but he would actually be working for her. He agreed and the plan was set in motion. The Iranian made it clear that he was not doing this for the money, but because of Kevin's motives. He said he wanted to see mother and daughter back home in the United States.

When Murat told Jodi that the attorney had agreed to help them, Jodi was shocked at the turn of events.

I didn't know who to believe. Was Kevin really acting that crazy?

She sat opposite Murat as he called his friends and family back on his yacht in the Mediterranean and could understood some of what he was saying.

"This is a case I cannot believe. A woman comes by herself to rescue her daughter out of Iran. Yes, it is crazy. People at the highest levels of both governments are working on this. I have never worked on a case with the FBI, the State Department and the embassy of the United States involved. I think I have a way now to get it done and get them back to the United States. You won't believe how it will happen." Murat paused to listen and then said, "Yes, I will be back to vacation soon." As Murat relayed his message to Jodi, he kept rubbing his forehead in disbelief.

Jodi's prayer that night was to ask God again to watch over Mari and let her tender heart believe that her mother was on her way. Jodi knew she had to trust Murat. She had been told many times by the FBI and State Department to, "Listen to your lawyer; he will know what to do."

Jodi and her attorney finished dinner just before 11 p.m. He said he was taking her back to the hotel and for her to be prepared to meet him at eight the next morning. He would then take her to see Mari.

"I want this matter finished, so I can get back to my vacation."

Jodi thanked him and watched him get in his cab and drive away. She quickly walked to the elevators in the lobby while replaying Murat's last words to her.

CHAPTER 25

MONDAY, AUG. 8
SHERATON MASLAK ISTANBUL HOTEl
(THIS IS NOT THE UNITED STATES)

As JODI STEPPED INTO THE elevator for the lift to her room, she realized that every muscle in her body ached. She was totally exhausted in body and mind, but not in spirit. She would finally be seeing Mari! The thought of being with her daughter again filled her with sweet energy. She leaned against the wall of the elevator and closed her eyes, just imagining Mari.

Mari will be so much taller now and her permanent teeth will be in. Will she recognize me? Will she want to run into my arms? Will she want to come home? My sweet energetic Mari, she always smelled like fresh linens and wild flowers.

Jodi entered her room and even though she was very tired, knew she needed to talk with Robby. She looked at the time and calculated it was early morning back in the states. She had tried to use the phone cards she purchased before leaving for Turkey, but they wouldn't work. She hesitated to text Mike to ask him to have Robby and Donna call her, but she felt she must.

Within minutes Robby called her back. She filled him in on what had taken place that day and he said that Mike was keeping him informed and of how sorry he was about all the ups and downs she was experiencing. He urged her to keep hanging in there. "You're doing great," he encouraged, adding that he had been in touch with her brother to let him know what was happening.

As she was talking with Robby, she consciously decided to only tell him what she thought he needed to hear and to keep Kevin's attorney's actions to herself, just as Murat had warned. "This is our business for now; no one else needs to know at this point."

It was hard for Jodi not to tell Robby what was really going on. He knew most everything about her and up to that minute, she had been very honest with him. Jodi realized once again that she was not in the United States and things were done differently in Turkey.

She thanked Robby for everything he was doing and hung up.

Her thoughts drew her to the window and she looked down at the bright city lights of Istanbul.

Somewhere out there my daughter is hopefully sleeping peacefully.

She prayed to God to bless Mari with sweet dreams and to let her know her mother was on her way.

Jodi knew Donna must be calling when she heard her phone ring again. She felt a need to let loose and allow her emotions to surface and knew she could trust Donna to understand.

"Hi Jodi, are you doing OK?" Donna said in greeting.

She knew Robby and Donna must have spoken with each other before Donna called her.

"No one should have to do this Donna. My God, this is insane! Let's see. I have been here all day and still haven't been able to see Mari. A machine gun was shoved in my stomach and everyone who comes in contact with me makes comments about how my situation must be like a sequel to "Not Without My Daughter." Also, I'm not too sure about my lead attorney!"

Donna just paused and being the calm, sane person Jodi knew her to be said, "Jodi, what you are doing is amazing. Mari is lucky to have you as a mother."

Donna knew just what to say to help Jodi feel better. She reminded her that nothing else mattered, except for getting Mari home. That simple comment did the trick and quickly calmed Jodi down as she felt exhaustion take over again. Even though she had already begged Donna, Robby and Mike to let the proper authorities know, she felt the need to beg one more time to make sure everyone knew about Kevin's repeated threats to harm her and Mari.

"Jodi, everyone is aware of Kevin's actions and the people involved have Mari's safety as a top priority. Get some rest and dream of seeing Mari tomorrow." Donna's voice sounded motherly and very soothing to Jodi's soul.

Donna's manner across the miles had a huge impact on Jodi. She disconnected the call and just hung her tired head as she replayed Donna's words to her.

Mari is lucky to have you as a mother.

By that time it was 4:30 in the morning and Jodi had to be up by 7 a.m. to get ready to meet Murat. She could hardly believe it was already Tuesday and that she had been in Turkey for 16 hours. No one would give her the address to the orphanage, but she thanked God they hadn't. She knew she would have walked there, no matter the hour- a dangerous and foolish thing to do. She would have done anything to be closer to her daughter. Everyone kept telling her not to worry, that they would get her there. She believed that they were afraid Kevin would be outside waiting for Jodi to be alone. It was amazing and so frustrating to Jodi to be on the same continent, in the same country, within miles of Mari, but not be able to see her.

She undressed and crawled into the luxurious bed, tugging at the tightly tucked coverings. Every bone in her body hurt. She was certain she was dehydrated and even though she was in great shape, her lack of sleep, topped by the extreme stress she was experiencing caused her body to continue to ache. The swelling in her hand had diminished and she took off the wrap and decided not to wear it anymore. It was a bother and besides, she didn't feel any pain in it. She looked at her misshapen hand and fell asleep thinking about all that had transpired within the last few days.

She vaguely remembered falling asleep and 45 minutes later, was abruptly awakened with the terrifying nightmare that she had suffered almost nightly since Mari was taken. The dream was always the same.

Mari is with her and Jodi can see Kevin, but it is dark and he cannot see them. She feels her daughter as she holds her and protects her. The dream sequence moves very slowly as Jodi keeps watching Kevin searching for them. Her feeling of anxiety in the dream is so intense, that it forces Jodi awake every time.

She decided that there was no sense staying in bed, because she knew she wasn't going to be able to get back to sleep. As she got out of the bed, her body hurt so fiercely, that she wondered how she would walk; however, thoughts of seeing Mari brightened her spirits and took away some of the pain. As she was preparing for her day, she just kept praying that God would keep her strong; that she could accomplish what she came to do.

CHAPTER 26

TUESDAY, AUG. 9, 2011
TURKISH ORPHANAGE, ISTANBUL, TURKEY
(REUNITED)

JODI TOOK THE ELEVATOR DOWN to the lobby and reminded herself that she needed to eat to keep up her strength. She felt exhausted, yet was energized with anticipation of seeing Mari later that day.

The hotel attendant had told Jodi that breakfast was offered to hotel guests at no additional charge and to just show her room card to the cashier. He said she should take advantage of it, because the breakfast buffet was always "magnificent." When she walked into the dining room, she recalled how he had pronounced magnificent, which made her chuckle. He was right, breakfast looked and smelled amazing. Fruits, cheeses and breads were all carefully layered on beautiful raised platters. The selection of meats included special fish dishes, kabob meat and what looked like to Jodi to be bacon. There was also an entire line of colorful juices; pomegranate, grape, orange, kiwi and blended varieties.

She looked around and could only think of how much Mari would have loved looking at all of the food and how it was so beautifully displayed.

"My little fruit and vegetable eater; She was the easiest baby and toddler. She loved all kinds of food and loved trying new foods," Jodi recalled.

"Please help yourself," an attendant invited Jodi, after she showed him her card.

She collected a small amount of food and chose a table. A waiter approached to ask what she preferred to drink and he soon returned with the tea she requested.

She noticed a man looking at her, which immediately triggered Jodi into guilt mode, thinking that he must know why she was there and was questioning how she could eat when her daughter was being held in an orphanage. Consequently, she could eat hardly any of what she had on her plate. Logic told her he didn't know her, but yet, the guilt of knowing Mari was in an orphanage and maybe without food, stopped her from wanting, or being able, to eat anything more.

Jodi stood and tried not to make any more eye contact with people as she walked to the lobby to wait for Murat. She carried her tea and slowly drank from the cup to savor every sip. The hot tea tasted so good to her; it helped her relax and to have a moment filled with happy thoughts of Mari.

She thought again of how tall her daughter would be. Would she still be able to fit on her mother's lap so they could read books together like they had done all of her life? Thoughts of Mari trying to sit still as they read books put a smile on Jodi's face. As soon as they would come to Mari's favorite part, she would squirm and wiggle and shout out the words she had memorized from the story.

She's something, my daughter is.

Jodi snapped out of her private thoughts when she saw Murat walking in through the lobby doors. She jumped up and as she walked over to meet him, he smiled and said, "Let's go see your daughter."

She smiled back and thought, "Maybe I misread him last night because I was so tired. He must be a good man. He is helping me get to Mari."

The apprehension she had felt last night seemed to fade and Jodi's thoughts, once again, were focused on her daughter.

Murat explained that they would not be using a police escort that day, as there were guards at the orphanage who were aware of Kevin's actions and had orders not to let him enter the building. Since they would be pulling right up next to the guards upon their arrival, Kevin would not be able to hurt them, he assured Jodi.

However, her thoughts were far from Kevin and remained focused on Mari. She felt as if her whole body was smiling. She had been aware of God's infinite power during her cab ride and it had made her feel she had whatever abilities she needed to complete her mission.

The drive didn't take long, approximately 30 minutes, as the orphanage was on the European side of Istanbul, the same side as the Sheraton Jodi was staying in. Yet nothing had prepared Jodi for what she experienced upon arrival; the building looking like a third world prison.

Guards were everywhere and high fences surrounded the facility. Exterior walls were painted a dull tan and much of the paint was peeling. It took her breath away to realize that it was the place her daughter was in.

She understood that guards and fences were in place to protect the children within its walls, but the scene was so much worse than what Jodi had imagined. The cab pulled close to where a group of guards were standing and stopped at the front entrance. A guard opened a door to ask why they were there. Murat confidently showed him documents and started explaining who Jodi was.

Understanding the situation, the guard gestured to them to enter through a gate. After they entered, the gate shut behind them, which startled Jodi and stopped her search of the grounds for Mari. Her heart was racing so fast, she couldn't pay attention to what the guard and Murat were saying. She just kept searching for her daughter.

Was she playing outside? Will she be laughing and playing with the other children?

Jodi's mind continued to race. Murat told her that they were all clear to enter, which brought Jodi out from her self-imposed trance.

She was told Kevin had been at the orphanage earlier that morning, having slept on a park bench located in front of the building. Jodi was told he refused to leave until his attorney met him there and picked him up. She assumed incorrectly that Murat had arranged for his Iranian attorney to pick him up and leave before their arrival.

She was informed that Kevin had tried to get in and the female officer in charge, referred to as general, firmly refused Kevin's request to see Mari. Kevin then called his attorney who picked him up in his vehicle and told Kevin that they had to be at a meeting at the prosecutor's office. Jodi crossed her fingers in hope that the Iranian attorney would not double cross them.

As they continued walking, the orphanage appeared to Jodi to be a very safe and secure facility. It started to look even better as she walked through a courtyard. It was old, but very clean, she noticed. They were escorted to the office of the general in the girl's section. To Jodi, the walk seemed at least a half-mile long.

Jodi was just minutes away from seeing her daughter! Only minutes before her nightmare would be near the end.

As they entered the building, it reminded Jodi of an old elementary school. She viewed long hallways with the walls covered with children's paintings. Their artwork was displayed proudly. People were also lined in the hallways and she saw several children walking with adults. Jodi soaked all of it in as she scanned the hallways for Mari. To her relief the orphanage appeared to be a happy place.

They were greeted by a very nice Turkish woman, who welcomed Jodi by holding both of her hands and smiling at her. The woman didn't speak, but moved her hand in welcome, ushering the group into the general's office. The general walked over to Jodi and said she was glad to meet her, adding that Mari was a delight and that she was looking forward to seeing her mother.

She instructed Jodi that they would visit first as Mari was being prepared to see her.

Impatience and anxiety made Jodi feel like her skin was turning inside out. The general looked like a young Tina Turner, the American singer. She was a beautiful woman, yet all businesslike and very protective of her "children." She went on to tell Murat and Jodi about the orphanage and how it functioned. She told them that it was up to her to decide whether Mari would be returned to her mother and who was allowed to visit the young girl.

To Jodi, it wasn't said as a threat, but came from someone who prided herself on doing the best job she could. Tea was brought in to the office, accompanied by a pretty tray of little pastries. The woman was very kind to Jodi and asked if she wanted any tea to drink. Her command of English was excellent.

"No thank you, I just want to see my daughter," Jodi responded kindly but firmly. The general smiled and nodded. Her response must have pleased her, Jodi thought, and Jodi's eyes began to tear up as she listened to the general talk about Mari.

Jodi was first told that Mari had done very well the past four nights.

"She is a joy to have here, but she is upset and wonders what has happened to her father and asks continually when her mommy is coming," the general said.

She noticed Jodi's tears as she was talking. The General knew more about Mari than Jodi did at that point, which made it difficult for Jodi to listen to her words.

"You need not to cry when you see Mari," the general firmly told Jodi. "She needs to see you strong. I have heard you are a strong woman. She needs to see this." She smiled, acknowledging she knew what Jodi must be feeling. The phone rang.

"Mari's ready."

Jodi couldn't exhale. It took all she could do to stand where the general told her to. The room now held many more guards and other workers had also gathered to watch the reunion. If the general didn't like what she observed, she had the power to keep Mari in the orphanage.

Mari really did belong to them now.

Mari, holding a woman's hand, walked into the office. Jodi's heart jumped in her chest and she thought that she might pass out. She stared at her daughter, who was staring back at her.

Jodi was shocked at her appearance. In more than two years, her daughter had not grown. If she was taller, it wasn't by much. She appeared so frightened, that it scared Jodi. Her shiny brown hair had been cut short to look like a boy's, so she could get through customs without being detected. She was wearing a pink T-shirt with "I love my mom" in Turkish printed on the front and a pair of blue jeans. The clothing was way too small to fit her daughter, but to Jodi, Mari looked absolutely perfect.

Mari looked straight through Jodi, with no expression. There was no recognition of her mother and obviously no excitement. She didn't remember who Jodi was and Jodi could feel her heart plummet.

I had to get her to remember and all my prayers to this point had been answered. God gave me the gift to know what to do.

Jodi dropped to her knees onto the tile floor to be eye level with Mari and so her legs wouldn't give way. Everyone in the room was standing quiet and still observing mother and daughter. Jodi didn't notice anyone else was even in the room at that point, as she focused on Mari and how to get her daughter to remember her.

"Mari, you are so beautiful." Jodi said softly. Mari didn't move.

With a mother's instinct, Jodi suddenly knew that Mari was afraid.

"You look so pretty!" Jodi exclaimed, as she watched Mari's eyes. (The worker who had walked in with Mari had stepped away from her to give her space and permission to react on her own.) Mari started fiddling with eyeglasses hanging on a lanyard around her neck.

"No, I'm not pretty, I have to wear these," Mari said, speaking softly and looking down at the little pair of glasses.

"Well, so do I," said Jodi, showing Mari her own reading glasses which were hanging on a chain around her neck.

Jodi heard a little giggle come from Mari. Her arms ached to just scoop Mari up and run and explain that everything was going to be OK.

"You really do look very pretty Mari, so very pretty," Jodi softly repeated.

"Oh, Momma," Mari said, with a little more excitement.

Jodi calmly asked her daughter how she was doing and Mari meekly replied she was fine.

"It's probably hard for you to remember who I am," Jodi ventured.

"No, I remember," then quickly asked where her Baba was and if he could get in where she was staying and take her away.

The fear Jodi saw in Mari's eyes forced her to lock eyes with the general, who shook her head "no." The tightness Jodi felt in her chest lifted and she looked back at Mari while confidently saying, "No, Baba cannot get to you here. The general has given me her word that she will protect you."

The room was eerily still as if the people in the room were collectively holding their breath. "Mari, can I give you a hug?" Jodi wanted so much to pick her up and swing her around. She wanted to smell her little ball of energy, but the child in front of her was not the daughter she had known.

Mari told her that "yes," she could hug her, in a very polite childlike voice.

Jodi leaned in slowly to take her in her arms. Mari didn't lift up her arms, but Jodi could hear her sigh. She was shaking with fear and her eyes were glazed over, not with tears, but with a great sadness Jodi had never seen in them before. Jodi continued to talk to her softly and slowly as she held her.

"I know this is hard for you Mari, but Mommy loves you and we are going home together. We won't ever be apart again."

Jodi could feel her daughter's little body start to relax. She could feel just how fragile Mari was, both physically and emotionally. As Jodi held her and talked, she realized just how much Mari smelled like fear.

"I have brought some things to help you remember, do you want to see them?" she asked.

Jodi took her daughter's hand tenderly in hers and together they walked to the sofa. Everyone was still observing the reunion, but to Jodi, it seemed like she and Mari were the only ones in the room. Mari unsure of what to do, allowed her mother to pick her up and place her on her lap. To Jodi, it was a very natural thing to do. Mari wasn't as sure and Jodi wondered how long it had been since someone held her on their lap.

Jodi began by pulling tangible memories from out of her bag. The first to come out was Daffodil, Mari's favorite little stuffed bear. Mari started to look at it, and then seemed to recognize the little bear. Jodi felt that seeing it triggered a memory and perhaps made her feel a little happy. Mari had ordered Daffodil to stay home from the trip to Iran and sleep with Mommy so she wouldn't be lonely without her.

Did Mari remember?

Jodi pulled out a small photo album she had prepared with pictures of Mari's grandparents, aunts, uncles and cousins, her beloved frog, Junior, and family events. Mari flipped the pages of the album herself and at her own pace, looking at each and every one of them as Jodi just kept watching and holding her. When she finished with the album, she looked up at her mother and slowly told her, "I thought I would never see you again, so I forgot what you looked like."

At that she started to cry a little and Jodi squeezed her tight and reassured her over and over that "nothing will ever make her feel like that again!" Mari smiled and just kept looking at her momma. Jodi was aware that she only had an hour to visit with her daughter and wanted to make every moment count, so she kept Mari talking to help her remember that she was her mother, hoping it would help her feel safe.

Murat received a phone call while Jodi and Mari were visiting. He looked at Jodi and said that it was time to go. He motioned her aside so that Mari couldn't hear him.

"That was Kevin's attorney. They are willing to meet at the prosecutor's office with us right now."

Jodi was in shock, she had just been reunited with her daughter and she had only been with her for 25 minutes at the most.

How can I leave her? She is too fragile and scared. How could you do this to Mari, Kevin? Why did you do this to us?

Jodi knew however, that she had to leave with Murat so paperwork could be done to get Mari back to the United States, where Jodi could love her forever.

Jodi returned to the couch where Mari was still sitting, looking at the photo album and holding Daffodil under her little arm. Jodi could see a small smile on Mari's face as she looked at a photo of Junior, her frog.

Jodi bent down on her knees to be eye-to-eye with Mari. "Momma has to go and do some paperwork. It is important that we do this so we can be together. Do you understand?" Jodi asked. Mari just stared at her. "Can I give you a hug?"

Mari fell into Jodi's open arms. She sighed so deep and loud it sounded as though all of the air in her lungs had been expelled. Jodi immediately noticed the smell of fear coming from her daughter again. Mari had never had an odor, but at that moment, she smelled dirty, sweaty and afraid. The smell of her took Jodi's mind to the dark place she had experienced the last two years and three months and she realized her daughter had lived it as well. It took all she had not to give in to the tears which were forming and to just run away with Mari in her arms. But she knew she couldn't.

Jodi took Mari's face in her hands and made her lock eyes with her own.

"Momma has to go get some paperwork done so you can leave here and then we can go home." She said it firmly and confidently, hoping Mari would believe her.

Mari pleaded with her mother, "Please take me with you now Momma – I will behave; I promise. Please don't leave me Mommy." Mari was begging and holding on to Jodi so tightly that Jodi thought she was going to lose control. She had never seen Mari express any sadness, anguish or fear before.

It took everything Jodi had within her to calmly say, "Mari, look at mommy's eyes. I am going to finish this paperwork and then come back to get you. Remember, we are in the same country now and I will be back to get you. This is a safe place for you to stay and I need you to be strong and wait for Mommy. I promise it won't be long." Mari nodded in agreement.

Jodi could tell that Mari's eyes were messed up, just like she had been told. She didn't know the reason for the glasses, but she could see a glaze covering her eyes. Tears were slowly slipping from Mari's eyes and Jodi kept wiping them. She took a scarf from out of her bag and wiped Mari's tears with it. The scarf had been a gift from Mari's Iranian grandmother to Jodi many years before. It was silk and very soft. After the tears were wiped away, Jodi folded the scarf and asked the general if Mari could keep it with her, along with her little bear, until she returned. The general agreed. Mari had Daffodil, wearing its little cap under her arm and was hanging onto Jodi's hand when the general asked Jodi a question.

"Before you go, I would like to ask you to purchase some gifts from the orphanage store for Mari's roommates because they tend to get jealous of children going home and when other children get gifts. Would you mind?"

"No of course not, I will be happy to. Can Mari please come with me and help pick out the gifts for her new friends?" Jodi said, knowing that she was pushing the situation so she could spend more time with Mari.

"Of course, that will be fine."

Mari's eyes lit up .They walked together to the store, which was just two doors down from the general's office. It was the first time mother and daughters were together and somewhat alone in more than two years. They walked hand-in-hand and quickly picked out little pink stuffed bears and candy covered chocolates to give to Mari's eight roommates. Jodi finally saw excitement coming from Mari while she was choosing the gifts.

As Jodi walked Mari to where she was staying, her arms full of the little gifts they had bought, Mari looked up at her mother.

"Thank you for coming Momma. I will be strong while I am here."

Tears sprung to Jodi's eyes and she fought them off, knowing she must remain calm for Mari to believe everything was all going to work out. She gave her daughter a quick squeeze and a kiss and whispered in her ear that she would be back to see her the very next day and that they might be going home. A member of the orphanage staff took Mari's hand and together they walked away. Jodi's stomach tightened and she struggled to breathe as Mari walked out of sight around a corner. Jodi felt frozen watching her daughter being led away.

Murat reminded Jodi of the urgency to get to the prosecutor's office. She was hurting so bad for Mari, that she started praying. He just stared at her and asked her if she did that often. She didn't acknowledge him and just kept walking and asking God to take care of her daughter.

CHAPTER 27

Tuesday, Aug. 9, 2011
Istanbul, Turkey
(Perfidy)

As the pair ran to get into a cab, Kevin called Jodi's attorney and said he wanted to talk with Jodi. Murat told him he was just about to see Jodi and they would call Kevin back in a few minutes.

Murat instructed Jodi to speak to Kevin on the phone but to not tell him she had just seen Mari. Kevin needed to sign the document stating he had no issues with Jodi taking Mari home.

The attorney dialed Kevin's number and handed the phone to Jodi. She didn't want to talk to Kevin, but after two years of playing his game, she was determined he was going to start doing things her way. Seeing Mari had put Jodi into a very strange mood and she was extremely angry. So angry at Kevin for doing this to them; the three of them had a great thing going as a family, which had worked for them. Now, she was certain it had been an act on his part, which made it all the more frightening. This was the end of that family and now it was time to heal Mari.

"Hello." Kevin's voice sounded angry.

"Hello Kevin," Jodi said, forcing herself to sound calm.

"Why are you doing this Jojo? She will die in that place. What have you done?" Kevin exclaimed as his anger escalated. "We will meet face-to-face and talk about this without attorneys ... Let's just finish this and get Mari out of there!"

Jodi was thinking very quickly. "You need to do the right thing Kevin. I'm on my way with my attorney," and without saying anything more, she hung up not waiting for his response.

As Jodi and Murat jumped into a cab, Murat started explaining to Jodi what he had told the Iranian attorney to do. He was to tell Kevin that the orphanage was a horrible place. He would tell Kevin that he needed to sign a paper releasing Mari to Jodi, so Mari wouldn't get sick or die while she was being held in the institution. Then Jodi would give him everything he demanded from her. Kevin would be allowed to see Mari to tell her goodbye and then he could go on his way.

They would all meet at the prosecutor's office where Jodi would confront Kevin and convince him to cooperate. Jodi was then instructed by Murat about the paper she needed Kevin to sign. If they could get him to sign the document, then all they would need were the judges' signatures that would enable them to go home.

As smart as Murat thought he was and as smart as the Iranian attorney thought their plan was, Jodi knew better. There was no way Kevin was going to meet her and just talk. She had betrayed him in his eyes. The United States government and especially the FBI were now in his business- Kevin would be out for revenge!

Jodi confided to Murat that she was afraid to be near Kevin; convinced that he was planning to harm or kill her. Murat had not met Kevin to see and understand what a strong and powerful man he was, and a fighter. Jodi knew there was no one that could stop him if he wanted to hurt her in any way.

"I will be no good to Mari if he kills me and we need to be smart about what we're doing." Jodi repeated.

"OK, let me take care of it," Murat assured her.

He pressed multiple numbers on his phone and even though he was speaking in Turkish, Jodi sensed with each call he made, Murat was becoming more and more frustrated. But why? He had appeared to be filled with confidence just moments before.

They arrived about one block from the prosecutor's office and Murat said he hadn't found anyone to hide Jodi while he met with Kevin. Jodi suggested she could wait in the cab and that they could communicate by phone. He looked horrified.

"Jodi, I don't know this cab driver and I don't feel comfortable with your suggestions," he said anxiously.

They locked eyes for a moment in a struggle of wills before Jodi broke the silence.

"I will be fine, I haven't come this far to not finish this with Kevin and get Mari home. Please go see how he's acting and we can work via phone."

The cab driver was told by Jodi's attorney that she was a very important woman in the United States who was assisting him with a case and that she needed to sit in the cab until Murat called him. Once he called, he would tell him where to take Jodi.

The cab driver kept looking into his rear view mirror at Jodi and nodded at everything Murat was saying.

Before Murat left, he took the driver's cell phone number, as well as the cab number. As the driver was making the agreement with the attorney, he looked happy and then smiled at Jodi in the mirror.

Murat pushed the cab door open and exited out to the dusty sidewalk.

Jodi sat nervously in the cab. Minutes passed and she hadn't heard from Murat. She watched people pass on the street going into stores and shopping. Small cafés lined the street and looked very inviting to her. There were little tables with linen cloths laid over them and fresh flowers, making them appear so attractive. People were sitting at the tables, laughing, eating lunch, enjoying each other's company. She could picture Mari with her, the two of them eating lunch and just enjoying each other's company at one of the outdoor cafes.

The temperature was very high and getting hotter by the minute. Jodi was wearing a light skirt, a short sleeved shirt and sandals and still felt like she was boiling in the back seat of the cab.

Thoughts of Mari in the orphanage and how she looked were distracting Jodi. She knew she needed not to focus on the present situation, but to just focus on getting them both home. The look of relief on Mari's little face when Jodi had assured her that her Baba couldn't get to her and take her away again, haunted Jodi's thoughts.

CHAPTER 28

Tuesday, Aug. 9, 2011
Istanbul, Turkey
(Weapons)

ABOUT 15 MINUTES LATER Jodi's attorney called her. Jodi could tell he was highly agitated, but was trying not to yell. "Do not come down here, do you hear me? Do not come here! Does Kevin carry a weapon that you know of?"

Jodi was shocked by his tone. Murat sounded shaken, scared and bewildered.

"How would I know that? I haven't seen him in years... why?" she questioned, now panicking.

Murat went on to tell Jodi that as soon as the Iranian attorney introduced himself and Kevin to Murat, Kevin started screaming at him.

"Where is Jojo? She said she would be here. Is she in this country? I want to know why she isn't here!" Murat said he explained to Kevin, that under the circumstances, it might not be wise to have them together at that time. Jodi was working on getting Mari out of the orphanage and that she would contact Kevin once he signed the paper. The new information enraged Kevin even more.

"He is an animal Jodi, I repeat – do not come down here! Keep your eyes open and you tell the cab driver to drive away, anywhere, if you see Kevin."

Murat asked to talk to the cab driver. She handed her phone to the driver and could tell he understood what Murat told him. The cab driver handed the phone back to Jodi and Murat had hung up. The driver gave her a half smile but the look on his face was different. Jodi noticed he looked a little more serious than he had before.

Jodi couldn't even imagine what was happening in the prosecutor's office. Forty minutes had passed and she was getting more and more anxious. The driver had started to chit-chat with her, using the little English he spoke. It was so hot, that she offered him one of three water bottles she had packed earlier that morning. He graciously accepted it and she then gave him a granola bar that Nancy had made her pack. He studied the English writing on the package and nodded "Thank You" to Jodi.

A police car pulled up next to the cab and from what Jodi could make out during the exchange, the officer was asking why the cab had been parked in the same spot for so long. The driver explained what was happening and promised he would move as soon as possible. The police car pulled away and Jodi knew she had been holding her breath the whole time. The officer had checked between her and the driver several times. Sitting alone in the back seat made her feel vulnerable and she could only imagine what he thought.

People at one of the café's started to gawk when the police car pulled up next to the cab. Then, a few more people started gathering near them on the sidewalk. Jodi presumed they were thinking that something exciting was about to happen. A couple of young boys, obviously curious, came and talked with the cab driver. She could understand enough to know that he told them she was a very important woman from the United States of America. Even though that couldn't be further from the truth, the cab driver had believed Murat and it made him feel important. It was obvious that he was enjoying his role. He would repeatedly smile at her in the mirror as he would tell his tale.

Jodi smiled at the boys as they curiously studied her. The driver turned around and pointed to his eyes and then pointed to Jodi's. She understood and held up her Nazar Boncurgu necklace which was tucked inside of her shirt and held it next to her eyes. The boys looked happy and nodded up and down. They thought her eyes were the color of the Nazar Boncurgu. She chuckled at their actions watching them playfully shove each other and walk away and every once in a while she caught them looking back at the cab, until they were out of sight.

More time passed and Jodi was getting very nervous about the situation. Her eyes kept roving the streets for Kevin and it was getting hotter and hotter in the cab. She decided to call Murat. Murat answered and told her to remain calm and to be patient. The plan was working, he said. He was whispering and Jodi was straining to hear him above the noises coming from the street. He said he would call back in a few minutes to give her an update.

The background sounds of a city are so amazing to hear. In Istanbul, when you closed your eyes you heard busy sounds - Busy cars on the road, busy people walking and talking, a mosque's prayer music playing and the sound of Mediterranean Sea boats coming in to port. It sounded almost magical.

True to his word, Murat called Jodi back within two minutes and said he had told Kevin and his attorney he was going to try and call her. It was a ploy he used to calm Kevin down, he said. Murat had confirmed Kevin was carrying a weapon, which was strapped to his stomach. The Iranian attorney told Murat he noticed it as well, but couldn't tell if it was a gun or a large knife.

Fortunately, one language Kevin didn't speak was Turkish. Murat and the Iranian attorney could speak it and organized a plan in front of Kevin who understood only what he was being told. Kevin knew that Jodi's Turkish attorney did not understand Farsi, so he had no choice.

Kevin kept up his demands to see Jodi. His last statement before Murat's last call was, "tell Jodi that if she meets with me, I will turn over Mari's passport and sign the needed documents."

Murat and the Iranian attorney thought it odd that Kevin would bring up Mari's passport. They knew that when he was at the police station at the border, he had said that he didn't have her American passport and that they were traveling under Iranian passports. Murat surmised that Kevin wanted to meet with Jodi so he could get his $10,000 and that she would need Mari's passport to get her out of the country.

Murat continued by saying he and the Iranian attorney agreed, that after seeing Kevin's strength and size, it would take only seconds for Kevin to get past them if he wanted to harm Jodi and they both believed it was his intention to do so. Murat said he told Kevin and his attorney that Kevin could go to trial to try and get Mari back, but would not win.

"Jodi has the whole United States backing her; she has hired the best attorneys in Turkey. She is going to take her daughter back with her to the United States," Murat informed the men.

Kevin became extremely angry, and voiced his threat to get revenge against Jodi.

Murat and Kevin were screaming at each other in English outside of the prosecutor's office and people walking by stopped to watch the argument.

"You tell Jodi she has no idea what she has started! This will be finished! I will get what I came for! You tell her to call me!" Kevin yelled as Murat walked away. Murat turned around and walked up to the Iranian attorney and in Turkish told him, "You tell Kevin to sign the paper that he wants Jodi to take Mari back to the United States and only then will I will arrange for them all to be together, to sit down and talk before they leave. Kevin will get what he came for and Jodi will get what she came for," Murat said.

"I will get Jodi to call him once he signs the paper; so tell him if this happens, there will be no more problems in Turkey."

The Iranian attorney repeated to Kevin what Murat had said.

"Go f*** yourself. Tell Jodi I will only give her Mari's passport if she meets me in person first." Kevin wasn't screaming this time, he had gone beyond screaming and Murat said he was so out of control his eyes appeared to be black.

Again, the two attorneys could not figure out the importance of the passport to Kevin. They knew an emergency passport had already been ordered, but Kevin did not. They believed it was the only card Kevin thought he had to play, at that point.

Murat said he didn't say anything back and just looked at Kevin who seemed ready to explode.

"See you both – and Kevin, Jodi is prepared financially to stay in Turkey for as long as it takes to get Mari out and back home. How long Mari has to stay in there is up to you. Jodi will win in court eventually. I know her now and each moment Mari is in there your chances of getting the "gifts" she brought you will go away! I don't think I have met a mother more determined to be with her child. You won't win this Kevin."

"They will call, trust me." Jodi's attorney said to Jodi still by phone. "The Iranian attorney is doing exactly what we have asked; he will convince Kevin to sign." Murat was confident.

"I have to go, they are calling me now," he quickly said, disconnecting their call.

Jodi put the phone back down on her lap and shook her head.

Was this nightmare about to end?

"Please Lord, let Kevin sign that paper," Jodi prayed.

Visions of Mari living in the orphanage created the tears welling up in Jodi's eyes. She knew her daughter needed her now more than ever and she just wanted to be with her.

By that time Jodi had been sitting in the cab for three hours.

After Murat had walked away, the Iranian attorney pressed Kevin to sign the paper, so his client could receive the money and gifts from Jodi, assuring Kevin that Jodi had brought them for him. The Iranian told Kevin again that he had been to the orphanage previously on another case and it was full of disease and sickness, something Mari could most probably not survive. Her demise would be on Kevin's head and no matter how much he hated Jodi and the United States, he said he knew Kevin to be a good father and would want the best for his only daughter. The Iranian attorney thought then that he had Kevin "in the palm of his hand."

However, Kevin became leery of his attorney and asked him why he had changed his mind about representing him. The attorney said that the Iranian Embassy had told him not to worry about legal fees. Kevin was Iranian and so they hired him to represent one of their citizens.

Kevin hesitated for a moment and asked him to call Murat. Kevin said he would sign the paper saying he agreed that Jodi could take Mari home to the United States and that there was no need to go to court to fight for custody. He would allow Jodi to take Mari home. But, he was not giving up Mari's American passport until he saw them, received his items from Jodi and could say goodbye to his daughter.

Murat and the Iranian Attorney agreed that Kevin was bluffing. They both knew his feelings were that he had been betrayed by both Jodi and Mari.

The Iranian attorney had asked Kevin when they first met, why he was mad at Mari. Kevin explained that on the train ride from Van to Istanbul, he had made Mari promise him that if the authorities separated them again, Mari would tell them she wanted to stay with him, her Baba. She was to say that she did not want to go back to the United States and that she hated her mother.

At the police station witnesses to the action of their separation watched as Kevin screamed at Mari, "Tell them, tell them...tell them you want to stay with me. You don't want to go back to America... tell them! Tell them you hate your mother and how she is a bad person."

The witnesses saw Mari turn her back on her father and fall into the arms of a woman police officer whose job it was to protect her.

"Fine, I guess you have made your choice... you will have to live with it!" He shouted at Mari.

This story was told to Jodi by the police woman whom she met at the Children's Police Station. It was also relayed to her by the attorneys.

Both attorneys agreed if the meeting took place, Jodi would be hurt or killed and Mari was in danger of the same thing happening to her.

CHAPTER 29

*Tuesday, Aug. 9, 2011, after 5 p.m.
Istanbul, Turkey
(A restaurant called Rumelishisari Iskele)*

Jodi's attorney found her still hiding in the cab. More than three hours had passed but she was safe. It was after 5 p.m. and they still needed to obtain signatures from two Turkish judges.

Jodi calculated she had been in the country for approximately 30 hours as she sat watching the road and passing cars on the cab ride back to the hotel. Murat was sitting beside her and talking to his network of lawyers to plan how to get the papers in front of the judges for their signatures.

After he got off the phone, Murat looked at Jodi. She sensed his movement and looked over at him.

"We have to get these signatures. Kevin looked and acted like a caged animal and he wasn't caged," Murat said angrily. He continued on and was very irate. "I can't believe I left my vacation for this, that man could have killed me and for what? To help you?"

His words started to alarm Jodi, but she thought the confrontation with Kevin had shaken him. Obviously Murat wasn't used to dealing with the law in this manner. She could tell he was very angry by the way he kept holding his head in his hands. She wasn't sure what to expect next.

"How your government could let you come here alone. This is insane. You better hope the Iranian attorney doesn't turn on us!" he practically spat at Jodi while making his point.

She just stared at her attorney, not sure how she should respond to what he just said.

I had this weird feeling in my stomach that something wasn't right but I didn't know if it was fear or a real observation.

Jodi prayed that her "Mommy Power" would sustain her. She was at the point that she didn't trust Kevin, or her attorney, and as nice as the general acted while she was at the orphanage, she admitted to herself that she really didn't trust her either. Lack of sleep and worry were fueling her fears and suspicions yet she was oddly alert.

Moments later, Murat received a phone call from the Iranian attorney telling him that Kevin had signed the document they needed, in front of the prosecutor. Murat got off the phone and said, "Kevin must really want the gifts you have brought him." His face appeared to soften as he announced, "Tonight we will celebrate!"

She honestly thought that Murat had gone crazy and she didn't know how to react to the change in events.

"Celebrate what?" she thought. "Mari was still in the orphanage and they still needed to get two more signatures."

"He wants to celebrate?" Jodi thought in confusion.

Listen to your attorney; he will know what to do.

The words kept running through Jodi's mind as Murat said he knew of a restaurant that he wanted to take her to and that they could celebrate there. He didn't ask if she wanted to go, announcing only that was where they were headed and that they needed to talk. Jodi knew he was a man who was used to getting his way and it was starting to give her an uneasy feeling.

The sense of confidence she had begun to feel, evaporated.

"Good Lord!" Jodi wondered would she ever be in control of her time. The delays seemed overly ridiculous.

Why would I want to sit and eat an amazing dinner in what he described "as the best outdoor restaurant in Istanbul" while my daughter was lodged in an orphanage surrounded by people she didn't know; most of them not speaking to her in a language she knew?

Thoughts of Mari kept Jodi's mind very busy.

The cab stopped and they stepped out into the evening air. Jodi didn't know how to feel as Murat's mood switch stayed on happy. She watched him cautiously as he guided her up a ramp and into the restaurant. He told the maître d' he wanted a table by the water and that he expected privacy. The maître d' looked from Murat to Jodi and nodded his assent.

As they walked through the interior of the restaurant, Jodi noticed that many of the people already seated were watching them walk by. Murat was walking ahead of Jodi and behind the maître d'. She was amused that as metropolitan as Istanbul appeared to be, her Irish looks warranted curiosity. It did alarm Jodi that Murat had asked for privacy, but at this point, her thoughts remained on Mari.

The restaurant was truly amazing. Beautifully appointed round tables lined the water's view and you could feel the breeze from the Mediterranean Sea. The restaurant had linen table cloths in multiple colors that dressed the tables and wonderful fresh cut flower arrangements were displayed everywhere Jodi could see. The fragrances coming from the kitchen were heavenly.

Since she had arrived she had been grateful a million times over, that in the past months she had taken time to study the language for hundreds and hundreds of hours. She could not speak it fluently, but could understand more than she had thought she would. It was like her secret weapon and she never told anyone in Turkey she could understand what they were saying. The strategy was definitely working in her favor. When the language was being spoken in her presence, she put a blank look on her face to make it seem she did not understand a single word.

Jodi and Murat were seated at their table and for a few moments, Murat just stared at her. His staring made her quite uncomfortable, but she maintained a steady gaze back at him, knowing from her studies, that eye contact was very important in his culture.

"How are you feeling?" he asked.

She rolled the question around in her brain for a moment and carefully chose her words, answering him very softly.

"I appreciate all that you are doing Murat. You were very kind to assign Elif and Varol to me in your absence. To face Kevin was not an easy task, I know. It has been a difficult journey to get my daughter back and honestly I am not up to a celebration. I came here to get my daughter and won't be celebrating until I have her safely in my arms," Jodi said, willing him to understand.

He said he understood and smiled at her, his eyes searching her face.

The waiter came by to take their order.

"Do you trust me to order for you? I have eaten here many times and I know the best dishes," Murat questioned.

"Of course, whatever you choose will be fine and I am sure it will be excellent."

She looked out over the water while he ordered several dishes from the waiter. All she wanted to do was to call Robby and tell him what was happening with Kevin, that he had signed the necessary paper.

Yet, Jodi wasn't sure what to tell him. How could she tell Robby what was happening after Murat had made it very clear to her, that it was just between the two of them. She wasn't in America.

"Do you favor some wine?" He asked politely in front of their waiter.

She looked at Murat, he was acting like he hadn't heard a word she said before. She was so sick of being there, that she wanted to vomit. Her vision of rescuing Mari had not included anything that resembled sitting at one of Istanbul's' finest restaurants, sipping wine and eating great food; unless that vision had Mari in it.

She tried politely answering "no," but knew that her tone had an edge to it.

The waiter asked Murat, in Turkish, where Jodi was from.

"She is American. She is the American here to rescue her daughter," Murat answered. It threw Jodi off a little to hear him say that. She wasn't aware that anyone other than the governments and those involved knew about Mari or her. She didn't comment on what she had heard.

The mood at the table changed after the waiter left as Jodi witnessed Murat's mood changing again.

Murat began tutoring her on what she was supposed to say to the FBI and to the U.S. Embassy representatives, as well as the United States government, or anyone she would come in contact with before she left the country. He sounded very menacing at that point and Jodi was getting more and more nervous. Then it came out at her full barrel.

"If you tell anyone what I am doing, I will tell Kevin where you are staying and I will make sure Mari does not get released from the orphanage! You will have to pay to get the signatures and it won't be cheap! " Murat threatened sharply.

Jodi could only stare at him and wondered what could possibly be happening now.

"I have other cases in this country to work on. Some cases involving children. I can't be known as the man who is bribing the other party's attorney to work for them, bribing judges for their signatures on documents. It is against the law here to do so," His angry rant continued.

"I have never been involved in a case like this!" He finished his declarations by just shaking his head.

Jodi continued to just look at Murat. She didn't know if he was having a break down or if he really thought he was in trouble.

Cash is King.

Murat kept repeating that Jodi must not tell anyone what they were doing and how it was being done.

"I have no intentions of ever talking about what happened here and frankly, I don't care. I want to get my daughter home and that is all I am here for," she said levelly.

Her very calmness seemed to alarm Murat. Jodi thought he probably had expected her to be a helpless female from American that would fall at his feet

Dishes started coming to their table; fish entrees, vegetables in oils, bread with goat cheese, fruit and wine. The food seemed to lighten Murat's mood and he switched from an attorney to a man interested in the woman before him. He was curious. He started asking her questions and wanted great details included in her answers. Where did she work? Did she own a house? Did she date lots of men, or was there one special man? It was the tone of his questions which alarmed her, so she put into practice what she had learned, which was to turn the conversation back to him.

Once she had the turned the conversation, Murat told her about how he much he loved his daughters, but that his marriage was one of convenience. He and his wife were bored with each other, but still very much friends. Jodi continued to stare at him.

Who cares!?When is this madness going to end? I wanted so bad to get back to the hotel and plan out the next day. I wanted to be discussing what we needed to do next. He wanted to celebrate and show me the city. I needed to talk with Robby.

Murat received a phone call and excused himself. He walked approximately 30 yards away from where they were sitting, down towards the dock. Jodi could see that he was watching her from a distance. Her phone rang and she saw that it was Mike calling.

"Hello Jodi, where are you?" he asked.

"I am at some restaurant that Murat wanted to take me to. I need to talk to Robby, now," she said with intensity. Within minutes Robby called.

"Jodi, are you OK? Everyone is a little concerned because we don't know where you are."

"I really am fine Robby. Listen, I only have a few seconds before he comes back to the table. I am at a restaurant called Rumelishisari Iskele. I know where I am on the map." Jodi knew she was speaking very fast.

"Murat is telling me strange things about what I can and can't say and acting very odd about what is happening. I'm getting very nervous around him," Jodi admitted.

"You need to get him to take you back to the hotel and I will make sure that Mike is aware of what is happening. Hang in there Jodi," Robby instructed.

She put her phone down on her lap, just as Murat was coming back to the table.

"Is everything OK?" he demanded to know.

"Oh yes, that was Robby from the FBI just checking in to see if I was OK and if everything was moving along," she said and smiled.

Jodi told her attorney that people from the FBI were at the hotel and that they wanted to meet with her as soon as she returned.

It seemed to make sense to him and he nodded. They finished their meals and she asked where the restroom was as they were walking out of the restaurant. Murat looked at her with suspicion. She could see it made him angry, but wasn't sure what he thought she was going to do.

She went into the restroom just to catch her breath and to find her balance again. Jodi splashed some water on her face and dried it. She looked into the mirror, an act which seemed to calm her down. Instead of her own face, all she could see was Mari's face at the orphanage with that frightened glazed look which was haunting Jodi to her very core.

I can do this, please Lord, give me the strength to be strong, very strong. Help me figure this out.

She walked out of the restroom to find Murat standing there staring at the door and looking very impatient.

"Did you make a phone call in there?" he questioned. She didn't answer immediately and looked at him like he was a crazy person. She stepped around him saying, "Your Turkish tea runs right through me," as she kept walking towards a cab. Apparently it was enough of an answer because he followed her.

She knew she had to take control of the situation and lighten the mood to get Murat to take her back to her hotel.

"The dinner was very good. Thank you for taking me there, I especially enjoyed the fish kabob. The spices on the fish were delicious," she said with enthusiasm.

She looked at Murat as he told the cab driver where he wanted to go. It wasn't the hotel.

"I want you to remember something. I could tell Kevin where you are staying or tell him where you are right now," Murat threatened again, staring her down.

"What Now." she thought. "What now!" She paused for a moment to gather her thoughts and calmly looked straight into his eyes, "I am here to get my daughter home. If you can't help me, then don't. I WILL do it, I promise you I will get my daughter and take her home."

"You will do as I say!" Murat forcibly said.

The cab driver looked in the mirror and asked Jodi in broken English if she was OK. The question shocked Murat and calmed him down.

They arrived at an outdoor tea garden and in another place and time Jodi would have loved experiencing the quaint shop. It was full of energetic people who were enjoying the beautiful warm evening. Most of them were smoking from Hookahs. The elegant way people smoked from them caught Jodi's attention as she followed Murat to a table. Murat had not spoken to her since being interrupted by the cab driver.

Istanbul at night was a happy and cheerful place, full of life, with people drinking tea and smoking from hookahs. She was quite sure that in this little café, she was the only blue eyed American.

They sat down and Murat was still not talking. He never took his eyes off Jodi and she could tell he was either studying her or trying to figure out if he could trust her.

The waiter brought them tea menus and he ordered for both of them. Jodi knew there was no way she was going to drink it; she didn't know what he had ordered and also didn't want to take the time.

"Are we going back to the hotel soon?" she asked as nicely as she could. The lack of her control over time was beginning to wear on her and her tone was a bit testy.

He only continued to stare at her. His silence was deafening. It alarmed her and reminded her once again she wasn't in America. Looking around she started to notice her surroundings and due to all of her study, knew approximately where they were. She used his silence for a time to locate markers and began feeling stronger, knowing she could get back to the hotel by taking a cab. She also realized that the hotel was about three miles away, a distance she could walk.

With renewed strength, she braved a question. "Look, are you going to take me back to the hotel or not?"

Her tone snapped Murat out of his trance. She had said it quite loudly, which was attracting stares from others in the cafe.

Before he could answer, Jodi's phone rang. Glancing down at her lap, she saw from the ID that the call was from Robby.

Thank God.

Before she answered, she told Murat that it was the FBI calling and asked him if she should answer the call. The question seemed to stop his anger.

"Yes, answer." Murat instructed.

Jodi did so and Robby immediately asked if she was OK. She knew it was taking too much time to get back to the hotel and he was getting concerned.

"Yes I'm fine. Oh, hang on and I'll ask him," Jodi said, pretending Robby had asked her a question. She wondered if Robby thought she had lost her mind.

"The FBI wants to know when I will be back at the hotel," she told Murat, as she continued on with her pretense. "Apparently, the FBI legat is there waiting for me to do some paperwork."

For the first time in what seemed like hours, the attorney came back down to earth. "Tell him we are leaving here shortly and that we're 45 minutes away."

She relayed the message to Robby, who for a moment didn't speak.

"Jodi, please text Mike as soon as you get inside the hotel. I will call you shortly after that. Hang in there," Robby said as he always did. But, it was the first time she had ever heard Robby's voice sounding as if he didn't quite know what to do.

She mentally thanked God for Robby calling at the perfect time. Just as in the past 800 days, Jodi was living one hour at a time. Now all she had to do was make it back to her hotel.

CHAPTER 30

WEDNESDAY, AUG. 10, 2011
ISTANBUL, TURKEY
("SHE'S VERY PUSHY!")

THE CAB RIDE BACK TO the hotel was very quiet and Jodi sensed that Murat knew that she no longer trusted him. He was right, he had threatened her by saying he would expose where she was to Kevin. Who would say that to her in her situation? Was it a scare tactic or was he really worried that Jodi would reveal the things they were doing to obtain the signatures for Mari's release? He didn't seem to understand that she had hired him for one reason only and once she did what she came to do, couldn't get home fast enough. Putting Istanbul behind her was top on the priorities list for herself and Mari.

After seeing Mari's condition, Jodi decided she needed to contact Nancy. Before heading up to her room, she sat down at one of the guest computers in the lobby, fired it up and logged into her email account. Her fingers flew over the keyboard as she typed the quick missive.

Nancy Reed
08/10/11 at 1:19 AM
<helloç

please tell mom and dad we are doing ok ı should get marı today no phone to make calls except to donna and robby thanks for all you are doing back there- not much tıme for access for emaıl- ı will get messages to you thru them after ı get marı and we are back at hotel- ı hope mom and dad are doıng ok - ıfyou can send me a message back tellıng me everyone ıs ok back there-

ı ask donna to get mom to get marı an appoıntment wıth debbıe- ı just want her to have an overall check-up marı wıll be more comfortable wıth a woman- ask her ıf ı can see her too

talk to you soon - love you all very much and cant waıt to get back to usa- thank everyone for all they are doıng for us-

marı was so happy to see me- she ıs so very beautıful- ı canıit waıt foryou guys to see her- she ıs so amazıngly brave

donıt worry ı am ok

love you all, jodı and marı

Jodi quickly reviewed what she wrote, not wanting to worry Nancy, but felt an urgency to have Mari and herself checked out by a physician once they were home. She didn't have time to correct the way the Turkish computer composed her text, but was confident that Nancy could understand it.

She closed down the program and headed upstairs to her room. She was so sick of being in Turkey and the associated drama. She just wanted to go home with Mari.

Once in her room, she sat down on the edge of the bed to think about what was going to happen the next day. She questioned if Murat would show up and if they could get the signatures needed to obtain Mari's release. She wondered how she could do it by herself if her attorney didn't show. She didn't know who Murat had been talking with to help him maneuver the task and did not know how to get in touch with Kevin.

It was then that Jodi remembered Robby and his request. She hurriedly texted Mike to say that she was fine and back at the hotel.

It was after 1 a.m. Jodi knew that she was totally exhausted and again every muscle in her body was hurting. She had to concentrate to even perform ordinary tasks. She lay on the bed and looked outside at the lights of the city. She just wanted to stay lying there and imagine Mari's pretty face and imagine them both home.

Her phone rang and she saw that Robby was calling. They talked for a few minutes and Jodi told him what Murat had said about what she could and could not say. She didn't tell him about Kevin's attorney working for them.

"I felt bad not totally confiding in Robby, but as I was told, this wasn't America. I knew that if I didn't do what I had to, Mari would have been in the orphanage for a very long time," Jodi mused.

She assured Robby that she would fill him in when she was back home. Within a few minutes, Jodi's phone rang again. She smiled as she picked up, knowing it was Donna who was calling. She assured Donna by telling her the same thing she told Robby - she would tell her everything, once she and Mari were back and that she needed to plan for the next day.

Jodi told Donna that she felt no parent should have to go through what she was experiencing to get their child back and that no U.S. citizen, no matter how young, should be held in an orphanage under Turkish control.

Donna listened, knowing Jodi was just venting and gently told her again, "Mari is lucky to have you as a mother, you are doing great and I can't wait to meet your daughter." They said their goodbyes, with Donna promising that she would update Jodi's family that they were doing fine and progress was being made.

The words Donna said about being excited to meet Mari filled Jodi with a renewed energy.

It was 3:30 a.m. Jodi sat on her bed, yearning for Mari. She pulled a chair next to the window so she could look out over the city and think.

Somewhere out there Kevin was wondering when I would call to set up the "meeting," so he could do what he planned on doing. Somewhere out there Mari was tucked into a bed in an orphanage holding her little bear in her arms.

Jodi imagined Mari sleeping peacefully which allowed her to plan. She continued looking out the window, allowing her eyes to roam the city, planning out her next day with or without Murat. She wondered again why Kevin was doing what he was doing. Why was he destroying the little family? Her thoughts angered her deeply. Ten thousand dollars, a computer and a set of walkie talkies was what he thought his daughter was worth. She stayed curled up on the chair by the window, still in the clothes she had worn all day, and watched the amazing city, active in pre-dawn hours.

Morning arrived and Jodi awoke, surprised to still be dressed and in the chair by the window. She checked the time, it was 6:30 a.m. Murat hadn't said what time he was coming, so she got ready and was downstairs by 7:30.

As she walked from the elevators to the lobby, she could see Murat sitting on one of the many sofas in the lobby area. He motioned for Jodi to sit down near him.

"So, do you want to see your daughter, do you want to get her back today?" He asked sharply.

Of course I do," she said without emotion while watching his every action.

"I have to make one phone call before we can go see Mari, but we need to talk first." He said more calmly.

What now?

"How much do you think a rescue like this is going to cost you?" He continued,

"I have done things I have never done before with any case. I am a good man with a good family." He paused and Jodi tried to jump in to answer, but he went on with his speech.

"I could stop right now and just tell Kevin that it is over and tell him where you are."

Again with the threats … focus Jodi … focus … answer very carefully… you need to get to Mari and Murat holds the golden ticket.

In the past days, she had asked Murat to see the needed paperwork. He would always tell her that it was in Turkish and besides, she would not understand what she was looking at. Jodi asked him if there would ever be any papers in English.

"This isn't your United States," was Murat's persistent answer to her.

"I will pay you exactly what you tell me to pay," Jodi slowly responded, watching his face for clues.

"Don't look at me and tell me what color my eyes are!" He demanded, changing the subject abruptly. Jodi thought he has lost his mind. What did his request have to do with anything?

Think carefully before you answer.

"They are green, but down at the water, they're blue," she answered.

Seeming satisfied with her answer he said, "I've brought papers for you to sign."

Jodi thought it was normal, expecting to sign papers; yet was surprised that he hadn't had her sign anything at the beginning.

He put the paper down on a table and pushed it towards her.

She picked the paper up to read the typewritten words.

I, Jodi Homaune of the United States of America, promise to pay _____ for the rescue of Mari Homaune, her daughter, and for expenses related to the rescue.

She was a little perplexed that it was so brief. It had his name printed with a line above for him to sign and Jodi's name printed with a line above for her to sign. A date was visible at the top of the document.

She wasn't sure what she was supposed to do. Was she to fill in any amount on the blank line?

"What do you think?" Murat prodded.

Answer carefully. This is like being in a bad movie. Fill in the blank the right way, or don't get your daughter back.

"I'm not sure what you want me to do." Jodi admitted.

"How much is it worth to you to finish this and go get Mari?" He said, staring at her.

Was she hearing him correctly? Was her nightmare ever going to end? All she could hear in her mind was Kevin telling her over the past two years, just how much it was going to cost her to talk to her daughter on the phone. How much was it going to cost her to see Mari in Istanbul? The two men did not get it – she would have done anything to bring Mari home and pay them all she could. So, here she was once again bargaining money to get to Mari.

Jodi knew how to play the game with Murat. She had done it for more than two years with Kevin. She decided in the future that it would be imperative to teach Mari about bullies.

"Maybe before in my life I couldn't spot them and had allowed them to enter my world, but not anymore and not in my daughter's life," Jodi vowed then and there.

She knew if she said an amount too low it wouldn't be what Murat wanted. On the other hand, she knew if she quoted an amount too high, it would come off as being ridiculous and disrespectful. Jodi racked her brain quickly to figure out the right answer. She thought he would be pleased with $25,000. This was money he wanted for himself. It had nothing to do with the cash that had already been paid out.

"I am not sure what I am supposed to write. I don't want to offend you, I just don't know what to write in here," Jodi said, trying to sound defeated. She pointed to the blank line on the paper he gave her.

"Umm, what is the price of a house in America?" Murat asked.

What was he after?

Before coming to Turkey, Jodi had dealt with Kevin on the telephone. It's much easier to deal with a bully by phone, she thought. Sitting in front of this bully and knowing he had the power to change things for Mari and her, was beyond scary.

She knew then $25,000 was not enough. Murat had told her he had been to America several times and she was certain he had a number in his head of what houses cost.

Be smart.

"My parents live in an area where the average cost of a house is $145,000," Jodi said calmly, searching his face for his reaction.

"That is fine, write it in and sign the paper," Murat said.

"Do I get a copy of this?" Jodi asked.

"Let's go, the police are waiting for us." He said sharply with a smile on his face.

She realized that he didn't have to make a phone call to arrange anything in regards to Mari. Jodi had just been manipulated, extorted.

She followed Murat out through the doors and saw the police chief in one vehicle accompanied by officers in two other official looking vehicles.

Murat ushered Jodi into the police chief's vehicle. He had a driver. The chief sat in front and Murat and Jodi sat in the back seat. There was a police car in front and another behind them.

Murat and the chief started to converse about the paperwork and going to the orphanage. What she understood of their conversation was that the chief was under the belief that they had obtained all of the needed signatures. Kevin had signed off and the chief said he was happy to have that taken care of. He asked Murat if it was all true. Murat answered that they did have Kevin's signature testifying he was not contesting Jodi taking Mari back to the United States and that they had two judges/prosecutors signatures and were waiting on just one more.

"It is being handled as we speak," Murat confidently told him.

The chief was instantly angry. "Why have you deceived me? I thought this was all taken care of! The general won't let the girl go without the signatures. Why are you wasting my time?"

"Why are we arguing? Everything's fine; he signed the papers," Murat said, obviously placating the chief. "She has signed her papers as well; all will be taken care of." He was almost cheerful.

As Jodi stared out the window, she caught the eye of the policeman who was driving. She could tell he had no idea what was happening in the vehicle and probably wondered if Jodi understood their Turkish conversation.

As they drew closer to the orphanage, Jodi could see the chief relax and he and Murat were soon discussing boating and football. It was a comfort to Jodi that their voices had calmed down and that she was being ignored. She was developing a plan about what to do if her lawyer double-crossed her and ended up telling Kevin where she and Mari were staying. She needed the time to think.

Before her journey to Istanbul, she had looked up the number to CNN, the television network in Istanbul. She had decided if she got into great trouble, she would call the station to tell someone what was happening. She honestly did not know if it would work, but it was something to hold on to. The number was tucked away in her purse and she made the decision that if the actions of the police chief and her attorney became threatening, she would stay in the orphanage and call CNN. Plus she could call Robby and Mike. She knew something would have to work.

Once the plan was firmly decided in her head, Jodi watched once again for familiar buildings she had studied to come into view. Jodi listened to the siren blaring above the vehicle. It wasn't an emergency, but because traffic was so heavy they were using it to cut through faster. She believed that the driver enjoyed the speed. He said nothing at all to his superior, but Jodi caught him looking back at her in the mirror often.

The entourage of vehicles arrived at the orphanage and Jodi noticed that they pulled up to a different guard house. The chief of police spoke to one of the guards to tell him that his group was there to see the male general, which answered Jodi's unasked question of why they arrived at a different section of the orphanage. She was told that the male general was in charge of the entire orphanage and that the female she had met the day before, was responsible only for the girls unit.

The guard solemnly nodded and Jodi, accompanied by her attorney, the chief, and three policemen and the drivers, all walked into the building together. The drivers stayed behind and began talking among themselves. Jodi thought it was interesting that all three drivers were in blue uniforms but their chief wore plain clothes, like he was undercover. She noticed that they were all wearing side arms and didn't smile much.

She had the sense that they thought this whole thing about Mari was a "pain in their butts."

The police chief stopped them as they approached an elevator, which would take them to the floor where the general's office was located. He motioned them to the side so people behind them could get on the elevator.

What now?????

Jodi was surprised at the strength of his arm when he stopped them. She looked directly at him when he grabbed her elbow and pulled the group aside. The chief turned his head to tell Murat that he wanted an American set of handcuffs; "Remington". Murat looked at Jodi, "Before the chief takes us up to the general, he wants a pair of police cuffs," he said wryly. Jodi thought she had entered the "Twilight Zone."

"What?" She firmly questioned. She shook her head slowly back and forth and asked again, a little more forcibly. "What does he want?"

The police chief looked angry and Jodi just looked at him.

What am I supposed to do? Think... think...

Jodi came up with an idea.

"Let me call my friend Mike who works at the consulate to see if I can get a pair," Jodi said as she smiled nicely. All she really wanted to do was throw-up in their faces. She walked a few feet away and looked over to see them chatting and laughing between themselves.

The bastards.

Jodi called Mike, as her hands shook. She was so close to getting Mari and had another hurdle to jump over with another insane request. Thankfully Mike answered her call.

"Hello Jodi?" He said, wondering why she was calling him. "Are you OK?"

"Mike, I am on my way to see the general to get release papers so Mari and I can get out of here, but the chief of police stopped me and refused to go any further until I can get him a pair of American handcuffs – some kind called Remington." She tried to sound as normal as she could, despite how ludicrous it sounded.

"Are you kidding me?" Mike retorted.

"No, I'm not," Jodi responded, while she kept her eyes on the attorney and police chief.

"Put your attorney on the phone. Hang in there Jodi, you are doing great. Hopefully it is almost over."

She walked over to the group of men and handed Murat the phone. Mike spoke in Turkish with Murat and then Murat handed the phone to the chief. Jodi saw the chief smile when he closed the phone and handed it back to her. She knew Mike must have promised to deliver the handcuffs.

While they were on the elevator, she looked around at the chipped paint and the size of the elevator and hoped to God it didn't get stuck. She, Jodi, from small town America, was packed inside of the outdated contraption with policemen and a Turkish attorney. A feather wouldn't have fit between the members of the group. The elevator moaned and they were in motion.

Handcuffs!

The elevator deposited the group near the general's office, which was the size of a small home. Artistic statues seemed to be placed everywhere and the windows overlooked a playground inside the orphanage grounds. The general's desk held many smaller pieces of art, as well as a vase of fresh flowers. In front of his desk was a sofa and two plush chairs placed on each side. A beautiful, glossy marble table was positioned in front of the sofa.

The general approached Jodi and shook her hand as he told her he was glad to meet her, before shaking Murat's hand.

"Please come in and be seated," he invited.

They waited until the general sat down and then they followed suit. It felt like being in front of a judge. The general looked at Jodi for several seconds, then looked around at the police team and then at Murat. It was hard for Jodi to discern what he was thinking about.

Jodi was feeling more and more anxious to see Mari and was becoming quite uncomfortable being surrounded only by men.

She had no idea what to expect and did not trust anything or anyone at this point. A woman came into the office carrying a tray of tea.

"Would you like some tea Miss Jodi?" The general asked her kindly.

"I only want to take my daughter home."

It was hard for her to even look at the chief and her attorney at this point. Her stomach was churning and her head spinning from fear that they would do something to stop her from getting Mari.

The general ignored her statement and the other people began talking to each other as if she wasn't in the room any longer.

"She's very pushy," said one of the officers in Turkish. Murat quickly came to her defense, reminding the small group that Jodi was a nice "American" woman.

Of course I was nice; $145,000 nice!

Her thoughts wandered as the men continued talking. She thought about how she could dial Mike without anyone else knowing and have him listen to the conversation. She hesitated to do that; she knew if they saw what she was trying to do, they might change their minds about releasing Mari, or worse. She really believed that they would harm her if they caught her doing something to undermine them and that no one would ever know what happened to her. They could easily pin the blame on Kevin. As she made the decision not to dial Mike, she looked down at the phone safely tucked inside of her purse, to make sure it was still there.

"They want to know if you play basketball because you are tall for a woman." Murat said directly to Jodi.

Are you kidding me?

However, she played along. Jodi told the men that she had played basketball when she was younger. Murat translated for her as she sat and smiled pleasantly at the group. They asked her all kinds of questions on basketball. Did she know Michael Jordan? How tall was he really? How many players did she know? She laughed to herself at what an insane conversation it was.

As the general was going through the paperwork he was given, he had found the first prosecutors signature releasing Mari to Jodi, he had found Kevin's signature stating Jodi could take Mari to the United States. He located one judge's signature and looked up and asked, "Do you have the second judge's signature?"

The police chief shifted in his chair uncomfortably. Murat positioned himself on the edge of the sofa to talk. The mood in the room became tense and Jodi could sense the change by the body language of the men. Even though she knew what the general had asked, she couldn't answer, because then they would know that she had lied and she did understand their language.

"No," Murat simply said.

Jodi thought her head was going to explode. No explanation, no confirmation that they expected to obtain the last signature; just a "no?"

The general stood up and spoke to everyone in the room. "Why are you wasting my time! Get out all of you!" he screamed. "Don't waste my time until you have the judges signature!"

A feeling of rage came over Jodi and she walked to the front of his desk and looked him in the eyes. Standing, the man was quite tall, so she had to look up at him.

"I am not leaving this office until I have my daughter and I am walking out of here with her! You can make them leave, but I will not!" Jodi said, nearly screaming herself.

Jodi walked back over to the couch to sit down, because she knew she was about to pass out. *What had she done?* She was shaking she was so angry.

"I think I just pushed too far," Jodi thought as she stared at the general. Her heart was pounding very hard. She ignored the feeling, knowing how close she was to rescuing Mari. Absolutely nothing was going to stop her. It was the final straw. The prior 802 days caught up with her at that moment. She was tired, lonely, scared and missing her life with her daughter. Money had been extorted from her steadily for the past couple of years, extorted from her this morning and just a few moments ago, extortion for a pair of handcuffs— she was completely ticked off.

All these people are preventing my daughter and me from being together.

She could feel the general's eyes on her, most likely shocked at her outburst. She continued to stare at him. Within seconds, Murat's phone buzzed and he answered the call. All eyes were on him, except for the general who was still staring Jodi down.

"I have it, no worries. I have the signature!" he said to everyone, waving his phone around as if that would bring peace to the situation.

A slow smile started to work its way across the general's face. He rose up and approached Jodi to stand over her. Not sure of what to do, Jodi stood up, as well. In her mind, the general was yet another barrier she had to break through to get to Mari. She was no longer afraid. Years of bullying had strengthened her and she was not about to back down. She felt more confident in her ability to rescue Mari than she ever had before.

Jodi looked up at the general when Murat started to talk. The general waved his hand to hush the attorney. Jodi could tell that Murat was uncertain of what the general might do.

"I would have had to remove you until I received the last signature," he said very slowly. His English was clear.

Jodi glared at him, a look that was in sharp contrast to her sugar sweet tone. "I will tell you again, I am not leaving without my daughter. I wish to see her now, so please sign her release." She knew she sounded very demanding, but then again, that was her intent.

Murat explained to the general that one of his junior attorneys was in a cab on his way to the orphanage with the signed document. During the 15 minutes they waited for the attorney's arrival, the general informed them that the female general had given him an excellent report about Mari's reunion with her mother and that Mari had not stopped talking about going home with her "Momma" to America. Jodi soaked in his words and then the general assured her that she was only moments away from seeing Mari again.

It seemed that tears were always at the ready during the past years. At that moment, she could feel them surfacing and she struggled to maintain her composure. She really did not have time to cry; to allow herself the luxury.

The attorney arrived and gave the precious document to his superior, who then handed the papers to the general. Jodi held her breath as she watched him sign the document that would release the custody of Mari back to her and hand it back to Murat.

"Thank you," Jodi said sincerely with a real smile.

The general smiled back at her and she then could see in his eyes that he actually was a kind man who had just been doing his job to protect the children in his charge. He lifted his phone to call someone and Jodi couldn't understand what he was saying, except for the word Mari.

"The general is getting Mari ready for you. She has been told you are taking her home." The general was smiling at Jodi and he appeared very happy. "I was told she is very excited. She is a good little girl and she is lucky to have such a strong-willed mother."

As they exited his office, Jodi looked back and smiled at him. She appreciated him more then he could ever imagine.

The elevator ride down was silent. She thought the police officers probably thought she was a crazy woman or that they knew she had nothing more to say. The old chipped paint in the elevator that had disgusted her during the ride up now looked just fine.

The small group had to walk across the facility to get to the place she had been with Mari the day before. Jodi knew where she was and she was walking at a pace that wasn't comfortable for the rest of the group. She didn't care. She was walking about three feet in front of them and she was certain they must have looked like a comedy act.

An American woman walks quickly, carrying her bags, while Turkish police follow her, keeping up the best they can, while trying to appear dignified. What a cartoon it would make.

Jodi could hear their mocking comments as they talked together about how she stood up to the general and what he really could have done to her. They mocked the fact that she had married an Iranian and they mocked how fast she walked. Her confidence in God was much stronger then the men who surrounded her and He was on her and Mari's side, so she continued to walk fast and smiled the whole way.

When she reached the door, the female general greeted her and told Jodi she was pleased that Jodi was successful in getting the papers so Mari could be released into her custody. "I don't know how you got it done so quickly with the courts, but I am so happy for you and Mari." She said kindly.

"Mari belongs to me again," Jodi silently sighed to herself. Signing over her rights to Mari to the country of Turkey had been one of the more frightening aspects of her journey so far.

For 10 long minutes she waited. She paced back and forth as the whispering of the policemen and Murat continued.

Ten minutes seemed like 10 hours at that point. She kept glancing toward the corner where she knew Mari would appear. Then, Mari suddenly entered the room.

Jodi ran to Mari and scooped her up swinging her around and around. Mari giggled and Jodi gently placed her down on her feet. A thought slammed into Jodi's mind, causing her to feel panic, even in the midst of her happiness.

We still have to get back to the United States.

She looked over at the policemen and Murat. She looked down at Mari and said. "Hang on to my hand Mari and do not let go of it."

Mari nodded in understanding and became very shy around the men, hiding herself behind her mother. Jodi could feel Mari's grip getting tighter and tighter and realized Mari was afraid of the policemen.

Jodi leaned down and said. "The policemen are our friends. They won't take you away from me,"

Mari looked up and nodded and Jodi could see tears beginning to form in her eyes. Jodi fought back her own tears and squeezed her little hand harder and started walking.

They reached the police cars and Jodi loaded Mari and her little bags into the middle vehicle and buckled her into her seat. The entourage started to move as Mari leaned close to her mother, who could tell how frightened she was.

"We are fine now Mari, we're fine. We will be going home soon," Jodi whispered in Mari's ear.

Mari responded by leaning even closer and started asking her mom question after question. With the siren blowing and the police and Murat talking, it was very loud inside of the vehicle. Mari was shouting out her questions and moving around a lot. Jodi thought it was excitement and nerves, combined with anxiety. She could tell it was bothering Murat and his conversation with the chief, who were talking about Kevin and his whereabouts. She was trying to listen, but she needed to be attentive to Mari.

Murat became agitated at what Jodi believed was the noise level and Mari's questions. He looked over at Jodi and Mari and said that if Mari didn't behave herself, he would tell her Baba where she and her mom were. He smiled sickly at Jodi. Jodi managed to control her anger that instantly rose at his cruel words. She gave Mari a tighter squeeze and a smile.

As to not appear as a bad person to Mari, Murat took off his sun glasses and handed them to her. He showed her how they collapsed down to nothing and with a quick shake they snapped into glasses once again.

Help me get away from these people.

Jodi pulled Mari closer and made her look out her window and whispered in her ear.

"Just a little further Mari and we can talk all we want. Would you like a piece of bubble gum?"

Mari smiled and Jodi pulled a piece of gum from her bag. Mari chewed her gum, leaning close to her mom while looking out her window. Jodi had her arm around Mari to protect her and didn't say a word to anyone but Mari on the way back to the hotel.

CHAPTER 31

AUGUST 10, 2011
SHERATON MASLAK ISTANBUL HOTEL
(VICTORY PARTY)

THE POLICE ESCORT DROPPED THEM in front of the Sheraton's entrance and Jodi politely said, "thank you" to the officers before walking quickly inside with Mari. Murat followed them as Jodi juggled their bags and told Mari not to let go of her hand. Mari looked up at her and nodded her head.

Mike was waiting inside the door and quickly grabbed some of Jodi's bags.

"Hello Mari, I have heard all about you," he said, greeting the little girl.

Mari slid behind her mom as Jodi thanked him. Mike then looked at Murat who was talking on his phone. Mike had a decidedly odd expression as he observed the attorney.

"Jodi, the women from the consulate are here and would like to talk with you, Mari and Murat to make sure everything is OK for you to leave the country," Mike informed her.

His statement caught her by surprise. She wanted to go directly to their room and call Donna to get things arranged to leave Istanbul. However, with Mari clinging to her hand and walking tightly behind her, she followed Mike to the table where the ladies were waiting.

"Mari it is so good to see you with your momma," the women said nearly in unison. "Look what we have done to get mother and daughter back together, this is just so glorious!"

Jodi looked perplexed. What they had done? She realized that they hadn't any clue as to what she had experienced in their city. They had no idea at what had transpired the previous days to get Mari out of the orphanage. They had no idea that Murat had her sign a piece of paper saying she owed him $145,000. She stood there in shock and listened to the dialogue. She never smiled except at Mari.

While they sat talking, someone from the hotel brought cookies and drinks to their little party. The ladies gave Mari some animal toys in a small purse and a bag of M&M's for her trip home. Mari graciously told them "thank you," yet still remained close to Jodi. Mari asked them if she could serve the refreshments. Jodi could sense she had an overwhelming need to please the people gathered even though she was nervous and afraid. She didn't want to eat the cookies or drink any tea at first and just kept looking at her mother. Jodi could sense Mari's fear and uncertainty and Mari was sensing her mother's.

She saw Mike take a phone call and come back with a strange expression on his face. He was locking eyes with her and Jodi wasn't sure what that meant. Something didn't feel right.

Before the call, he had been talking with her attorney. They were speaking in Turkish and all Jodi could make out was that they were talking about Jodi's bill. Jodi's attention was focused on Mari and couldn't grasp all words that they were saying. The ladies were busy watching Jodi and Mari interact and commenting on how happy Mari looked.

Mike told Jodi that Robby would be calling her shortly. She looked at Murat and wondered what was happening, but he avoided her questioning look and started fiddling with his tea.

Shortly, her phone signaled Robby was calling.

"Hello Robby, what is going on now!" she questioned.

"Just listen Jodi. Your attorney is telling Mike that he hasn't received any money from you and he is thinking about filing fraud charges against you. If he does, they will put Mari back in the orphanage and you will be jailed until it is all straightened out. Murat will not tell Mike how much you owe him. Do you know what he is talking about?"

Jodi's heart sank.

How could this be happening? Dear God, how much more can Mari and I take?

Jodi closed her eyes for just a second and felt God's strength.

"I will call you back, or Mike will in just a minute Robby," she said.

"Mari, Mommy needs to go sit over there. See that spot by the plant? You will be able to see me. You can be by Mike and the ladies as mommy talks with Murat. You will be fine," Jodi said softly, yet firmly. Jodi made eye contact with the state department ladies and transmitted her confidence that they would keep Mari safe while they were separated.

"Murat, I need to speak with you privately," she said as she stood and asked Mike to watch Mari. He nodded even as his expression questioned what was going on. Murat stood up and followed her.

Jodi forced Murat to stand with his back to the "celebration party," so she would not lose sight of Mari.

Jodi's tone of voice was not one Murat had ever heard before.

"The FBI has just informed me that you are filing fraud charges against me, saying I was not going to pay you. He said you won't tell him how much I owe you."

"No, that is not true," Murat said, acutely embarrassed that she knew. He quickly added, "That is not what I said!"

Murat went on to say what he had said was that he had the option to file fraud charges against her for not paying him everything she owed. He said he didn't have to tell them his fee, because it was none of their business.

Jodi reminded him that when they had first spoken on the phone, he was on speaker phone. Her brother and sister- in-law were listening as Jodi explained to him she had spent all of her money to get to this point and she would have to make payments after returning home and started working again.

"You agreed!" and reminded him that his exact words were, "Let's get your daughter home and we will work out the finances later."

Jodi was truly sick of Turkish men at this point. No, not just Turkish men, but all men in general! She told herself for the umpteenth time that she just needed to get back to the United States. Her thoughts made her feel even stronger as she stiffened her spine even more and faced him down. Murat just starred at her. Jodi was keenly aware he was trying to double talk her into thinking that she was the one who misunderstood.

Before he could speak, she said, "If you go back to the table and tell Mike that we are good and we have a deal worked out and that I am going to pay, then I will keep your secret of what you say I owe you. Can you imagine what the United States government and the FBI would think about you if I told them about your $145,000 bill? Four days. $145,000! I signed your paper and I will keep my word. Make sure you get me a copy of that document."

Jodi walked away and left Murat standing where he was. Mike had kept his eye on Jodi and watched her go back to her daughter. Mike asked the ladies to remain quiet.

"Is everything OK?" he asked Jodi.

She responded calmly as she looked down at Mari. "Everything is fine, just fine. You can tell Robby everything is just fine."

Murat came back to the table and relayed the same message to Mike. Mike looked perplexed and walked away from the table to make a call. Jodi looked down at her phone and saw it was Robby again as Mike was walking back to the table.

"Hello?"

"Jodi, I just got off the phone with Mike, is everything going OK with your attorney?" Robby asked rather quickly.

Jodi looked up from her daughter to look directly at Murat.

"Yes Robby, everything is fine. Murat knows I will make payments when I get back home. The amount of my bill with Murat is our business and doesn't need to be discussed," she said confidently. She could see

Murat's satisfaction with the words she chose to speak to Robby and told her agent that she would talk to him later.

"Mommy, my feet hurt really bad," Mari told her mother almost whispering.

Jodi looked down at her daughter's feet and realized the yellow flowered canvas shoes she had been wearing were too small. Her little feet looked puffy and red. Jodi immediately took the brown leather sandals off from her own feet, removed Mari's shoes and replaced them with her sandals.

"What about your feet Mommy?"

"I will be fine Mari," Jodi said, winking at her. She turned to the people seated around the table and said, "I am sorry, but my daughter and I are leaving now. We are headed up to our room. Mike, can I call you later to work out the details about our travels tomorrow?"

Mike nodded and smiled. Jodi thanked the ladies of the state department and looked at Murat and politely thanked him for his services, as well.

Barefoot, Jodi walked with daughter in hand. Mike asked if she needed help with her bags and she said, "I've got this." She felt she was smiling with every cell in her body.

The pair got onto the first elevator that opened and Jodi sighed with relief. She watched Mari gazing upon all of the buttons on the elevator. In 24 hours, they would be on a plane headed back to the U.S.

Jodi opened the door to their room and Mari walked in. Mari was moving slowly and it appeared to Jodi that her feet still hurt. She placed their backpacks on the floor next to the bed and turned to look at her daughter. Mari looked back at her shyly and then ran at her, tackling her. They fell on the bed together, dissolving in laughter.

"I love you Mommy, thank you for getting me!" Her English was broken and her Iranian accent was very heavy. The feeling in that moment of having Mari back in her arms, just the two of them, wrapped in an embrace, meant everything to Jodi. Her world was right again.

As they rocked on the bed together with Mari sitting on her mommy's lap, Mari began to cry and begin to spill all that was troubling her. "Mommy I have things to tell you, things you won't like or want to hear." Mari's voice changed from sounding like a little girl to sounding very grown up. It was not the same sweet child's voice that had said "I love you Mommy," minutes before.

"My Baba beat me." She said matter-of-factly. Tears welled up in her big brown eyes and Jodi quickly hugged her tightly again and just let her sob. She rubbed Mari's back and rocked her back and forth as Mari's cries poured out her anguish of two years and three months of being separated from her mother.

"It will never happen again little one, Mommy will make sure of that," soothed Jodi. She tried to sound strong and sure but couldn't keep the sadness out of her tone. She knew the happy six-year-old who had looked so forward to meeting her Iranian family, was not the same child she was now holding in the hotel room in Istanbul.

Jodi's heart was breaking again and it actually physically hurt. How many times had the FBI asked her if Kevin would ever hurt Mari? In the beginning, Jodi attested that "he loved his daughter and that he would even take a bullet for her." His actions had to be about Jodi and the United States, not Mari. After the threats began Jodi got scared. She was panicked that he would actually carry out his threats, yet hung onto her belief that he would never really hurt Mari.

Now it was almost more than she could bear, hearing the truth as Mari's words and sobs continued. The horror of the last 2 years and three months was so much worse than anything Jodi had imagined.

In that protective embrace, mother and daughter spent about 40 minutes communicating. Mari spilled the horrors of her life in Iran with her father. She talked about some good things and then would share terrible stories about how she was treated as an American girl living in Iran.

Jodi "cried on the inside", but knew Mari needed to see her mother's strength and love. She needed to know that her mother would never

ever let it happen again. "Incredible," she thought, recognizing that her own mother had shared that same strength with her when Mari had been abducted.

How about taking a nice bubble bath?" Jodi suggested. "It will make you feel wonderful again and I have bubbles and little animals for you to play with."

Mari grinned at the thought. Jodi went into the bathroom to start her bath water. She had thought she could handle Mari's words but her tears started to flow. Thoughts running through her mind were coming in so quickly, she couldn't stop them.

That is why Kevin didn't allow me phone contact with Mari, she would have told me about the beatings. In spite of everything that was going on, I never ever would have believed Mari's own father, would have beat her.

As she walked out of the bathroom, she saw Mari sitting at the desk intently writing on a piece of paper. When Mari saw her mother, she got up and handed the note to her Mom.

Jodi read the note. "Mama I love you" was written in Mari's childish scrawl, accompanied by a giant heart.

It was beautiful, so very beautiful. Jodi picked up Mari and realized again that Mari had not grown during her time away. It worried Jodi, but she tried to put it out of her mind for now and carried her to the tub.

While Mari was taking her bath, Jodi used the time to empty Mari's backpack and make calls to Robby and Donna. Mike had told her as they left that Donna had already arranged a flight out the next morning and that she and Robby would be calling Jodi that evening.

Jodi began unpacking the items from Mari's backpack while listening to Mari, who was singing in the tub.

"I just can't believe, I just can't believe, I just can't believe," Mari sang softly like she was telling a story.

For a minute, Jodi sat still and just listened to her daughter's voice. Mari continued to sing her little four word song over and over again.

Jodi walked into the bathroom and looked at Mari lining up her little animals on the edge of the tub and swatting them into the water. Bubbles were everywhere and Mari looked up and smiled at her.

Jodi got down on the edge of the tub, started washing Mari's feet and asked Mari what her song was about.

Mari shouted. "I just can't believe you came to get me!"

Jodi remembers thinking at that moment how amazing it is what the human body and spirit will endure, and can do, for love.

Jodi helped Mari out of the tub and wrapped her in a Turkish robe. She placed her on the bed to watch Turkish cartoons, as Jodi tried to assemble what clothes Mari had with her. Jodi had been told by the staff at the orphanage that they had given Mari clothes to wear. It hadn't dawned on Jodi at the time that it was because she had nothing with her.

Jodi had assumed it was because Kevin was holding Mari's things along with her passport, and wasn't going to give them up until he got what he wanted. As she opened the bags, she realized that they were the same clothes Mari had left with.

Mari said she had packed all of her things to come to Turkey. As Jodi pulled out the items, she discovered the same swimsuit she had left with and the same underwear. There were no other clothes with her except a little skirt and some rags that were her tops.

The clothes Mari had worn from the orphanage smelled so bad that Jodi put them in an extra plastic bag she had brought. As she continued going through her bag, she found the *National Geographic* magazine that she had sent with Mari for her plane ride to Iran. It was in shreds, torn, ripped and stripped of even looking like a magazine. Mari could sense Jodi's questioning the way the magazine looked and said, "That is the magazine you gave me Momma when I left. I kept it all this time because you gave it to me. Sometimes I hugged it to feel you." She gave Jodi a happy smile.

Jodi smiled back, marveling at her daughter who had already turned back around to watch cartoons. Jodi placed the magazine in her brief case and couldn't decide if she needed to cry or just put all of the crying business on hold until she could get them home. She decided on the latter.

Jodi assembled an outfit for Mari to wear home from one of her own sweaters and tank tops. She added the little skirt she had found in Mari's backpack. She was hoping that the airport would have a shop which sold sandals or shoes to find Mari a pair to wear on the trip home. She felt grateful that the orphanage had provided Mari with what shoes it had.

It was nearly 8:30 p.m. and Mari must be starving, Jodi thought. She was once again sitting on the bed wrapped up in the Turkish robe and Jodi thought she looked so tiny.

They didn't dare go out of the hotel, so she glanced at the room service menu and found that the cheapest thing listed was spaghetti with meatballs. Jodi found that funny, but it was what it was.

She called in the order and asked them if she could pay with cash when it arrived, because she didn't want to use her credit card that was on file. She placed her order and looked into her wallet. She had exactly five $20 bills. One hundred dollars to get them both home. The thought gave her a little jolt of tension and she hoped it would stretch half-way around the world. Istanbul had been the final step in using all of Jodi's financial resources.

She looked over at Mari lying on her stomach with her hands on either side of her chin watching cartoons. She smiled thinking, "OK, you have come this far. One hundred dollars - spend it wisely. Food for Mari…wise."

Every little noise was making Jodi jump as her protection mode stepped in. She had to get Mari out of Turkey. Her thoughts at that late hour were on Kevin. She knew that he believed there would be a hearing at the prosecutor's office the next day when he would be able to see Jodi and Mari, get his requested items, and say his goodbyes.

She had made a phone call to Kevin earlier that day.

"Kevin this if Jodi… just listen to me. There is going to be a hearing tomorrow to try to release Mari. Once I have Mari, I will meet you at the prosecutor's office and allow you to say goodbye and give you the things you requested. Your attorney has all of the details." Jodi felt no guilt, telling him the lie.

She had made the call right after they acquired the head general's signature. Murat had prompted her to call Kevin. At the same time, he was on the phone with Kevin's attorney telling him what to do and say. The police officers were standing a short way from her and Jodi was sure they were talking about the new handcuffs that were coming

"Istanbul, Turkey," Jodi thought as she looked out the windows and glanced back at Mari.

What a journey this has been.

Her mind was swimming with thoughts about how much she loved her little girl. And how much they needed to get on a plane and fly out of there before Kevin discovered they were gone.

The dinner had cost $20 with the tip, which left them with $80.

Eighty dollars left to get home.

She knew that they could do it; she just needed to board the plane the next day without any hurdles. Jodi had already received Mari's temporary passport at the meeting earlier that evening and several documents from the United States Embassy stating why Mari was in Turkey. She was also provided with other documents to help them exit Turkey without a lot of questions.

The little dinner arrived on a beautiful tray that made Mari's eyes light up.

"This is beautiful Mommy, is this all for me?" She asked with smiling eyes. Mari's mood changed when she asked her mother where her dinner was. Jodi told Mari that she wasn't very hungry and that she would eat what Mari didn't finish. The truth was that she hadn't wanted to spend money for two dinners; sharing one would have to work.

Mari gobbled up the noodles, salad and bread. She ate like she was starving and it shocked Jodi to see her eat so crudely with her hands.

In time, things will get back to normal.

Thankfully the portions were large, so Jodi ate what Mari couldn't. They both ended up full and satisfied.

After they finished eating, they placed the tray on the desk and crawled into bed. Mari was exhausted, but was still excited. It reminded Jodi of their last night together in Virginia. What Mari had told her earlier about her experiences in Iran was weighing heavily on Jodi, however. Sleep would be difficult for her but she could tell Mari was drifting off as she rubbed her back. Mari giggled now and then and Jodi would ask her what she was giggling at. Mari just kept repeating. "I just can't believe, I just can't believe."

Jodi's phone rang and she saw that it was Robby calling. His voice sounded very different than it had earlier; he sounded relieved.

"How are you and Mari doing Jodi?"

"We're doing great Robby, but there are a few things we'll need to talk about later. Mari's life in Iran wasn't what we thought," was all she reported to him at the time.

"Mari is getting a back massage and is curious as to who I'm talking with," Jodi added.

"Mari, do you want to say 'Hi!' to Robby? He's the man that has helped us for the past two years," she said, as she handed the phone to her daughter.

"Hello?" Mari said meekly.

Jodi put the phone on speaker so she could hold it next to Mari and keep rubbing her back. "Hi Mari, it is so good to hear your voice. I hear you are getting a back rub, how nice," Robby said.

Mari nodded and snuggled closer to her mother.

Jodi spoke more softly then. "Robby we are good; we just need to get home."

Robby continued to talk and informed her that Mike would pick them up at 7:30 in the morning and take them to the airport.

"Everything is set. Just go to Customs and present the documents and passport for Mari that you were given by the embassy and State

Department. The people in Customs will believe her passport was lost and that is why an emergency passport was issued. Mike is going to stay with you and Mari until you get through Customs and into the terminal. Once you get to the terminal everything will be fine."

Jodi thanked Robby for being her agent for the "millionth" time and reminded him to make contact with her family and tell them that they were both doing well.

As soon as she hung up, Jodi knew that Robby would be calling Donna and then Donna would call her. "How I adore them," Jodi thought to herself.

"Hi Jodi, how's Mari?" Donna's voice also sounded relieved.

"She's so beautiful. I have a few concerns but overall I think physically, she's doing fine. I've sent an email to Nancy to have my mom arrange doctor appointments for us. Her life in Iran wasn't what we thought, but I will tell you all about what she has told me once we get home."

"Donna, will you ask Nancy to buy underclothes for Mari? I can get more once we're back home. She has nothing and the few things I had purchased to leave for her at the cabin are way too big. "I'm afraid she hasn't grown much and it worries me," Jodi said, emotionally. What had her beautiful daughter endured that hadn't yet been told?

"Of course Jodi, please don't worry. With all the love that you have for her, she will grow. Have a safe flight tomorrow and we'll talk again soon. Give Mari a big hug from me and hug yourself, you've accomplished something great."

After she hung up, so many thoughts kept running through Jodi's mind. She leaned down and hugged Mari for Donna and kissed her on her little head and then hugged her again.

Jodi knew she wouldn't be sleeping that night and she was OK with that. Her "Mommy Power" was full speed ahead and she was ready to get out of Istanbul.

Mari woke up about every 15 minutes that night, jumping in her sleep and then waking and checking to make sure her mother was still there. Mari's fear made Jodi's heart ache again and questions without answers were racing through her mind.

How could this have happened? Every parent and child's nightmare had occurred in their lives. Does life become normal after this; and what would become their new normal?

Jodi wondered what Mari remembered about her life in the United States. She thought about what the reunion with her parents, Mari's grandparents, would be like. She hoped that by now they knew Mari was out of the orphanage and they would soon be on their way home. She knew both of her parents would be praying "around the clock."

With a mother's heart, Jodi knew they would all get back on track, that it would just take time.

CHAPTER 32

THURSDAY, AUG. 11, 2011
ATATURK AIRPORT; ISTANBUL TURKEY
(MORE QUESTIONS)

THE NEXT MORNING MIKE ARRIVED at the hotel and called Jodi's room. Mari was awake and watching her mom finish packing. Jodi had risen earlier and was already dressed and ready to go, having kept the bathroom door open so she could hear Mari if she needed her.

"Thank you for coming to get me," said Mari in a little voice. Jodi looked over at her and saw tears coming down her face again as she looked out a window. She was dressed in her makeshift outfit and looked like a little old woman to Jodi, an old woman who was wearing a skirt and Jodi's sweater and sandals. She looked adorable. Her hair was clean and she had asked her mother if she could make it look pretty. Jodi told her it already looked very pretty, but Mari didn't believe that. Her Baba had cut her hair with scissors before they left Iran, after she had begged him not to. It answered the question in Jodi's mind about the misshapen haircut. Jodi assured Mari she looked adorable and beautiful.

Jodi wasn't sure why the tears were flowing and went to embrace Mari.

"What is the matter Sweetie?" she questioned, holding her daughter in her arms.

"I didn't think I would ever see you again," Mari answered.

Jodi knew Mike was waiting for them downstairs and that they needed to get going, so she reassured Mari once more that it wouldn't ever happen again. As she spoke the words, she prayed that Murat wouldn't change his mind about pressing charges against her. She worried Kevin would find them before leaving the airport. She worried the Iranian attorney would betray them about what they had done. She was concerned that the State Department, Mike and others would question her as to how she obtained the needed signatures so quickly.

I have to get back to the United States before I have to answer the questions.

She hoped the nightmare of what had happened would just fade away.

Mike drove Jodi and Mari to the airport and walked mother and daughter all the way to passport control. He stopped just outside of the area, but where he could still keep an eye on the pair. Jodi and Mari snaked through the line where their passports would be inspected. Finally, it was their turn and they found themselves standing before a large Turkish man, sitting behind a table. Jodi, while still holding onto Mari's hand, handed both of their passports to the officer. He stared at them after opening Mari's passport.

"Why isn't the child's passport stamped to tell us when she arrived?" he questioned.

Jodi explained that Mari had been missing and had been held in Iran. She explained that she had worked with the Turkish government to get her daughter back to the United States. She maintained eye contact with the man in charge, yet was keenly aware of guards that had come to surround her and her daughter; one on each side and two behind. Mari's hand was slipping away from Jodi's grasp, sweaty and weak. Jodi tightened her grip. She didn't know what was happening and wondered if the attorney had pressed charges against her. The guard was not happy with the emergency passport and the explanation Jodi was giving him. As more guards gathered, Jodi looked down at her daughter.

"Are they going to take me again?" she heard Mari ask with tears in her eyes.

"Don't worry. Don't let go of my hand." Jodi leaned down and whispered to her daughter. "They're not going to take you. You're safe, you're with Mommy." Jodi could see Mari was turning white with fear. The panic in her eyes frightened Jodi "You're safe Mari; I am not going to leave you." Jodi repeated. She prayed that the ordeal would soon be over.

Not knowing what to do, Jodi looked over to where she had last seen Mike to let him know she needed help. Mike must have seen what was happening and was already approaching the guards. He addressed the large man in Turkish. Their conversation began to get louder and louder and people started to stare.

After listening to the officer's response, Mike told Jodi that the guard thought she was kidnapping Mari. Mike corrected the guard and an argument broke out between them. Despite his diplomatic demeanor, Mike couldn't seem to make them understand. Their voices escalated in volume until it was actually a shouting match.

Mike finally convinced the guard to get someone from the U.S. Embassy on the telephone. After what seemed like a long time, the Turkish ambassador to the U.S. talked with the guard and verified Jodi's account. Thirty-minutes had passed and Jodi worried that they had missed their flight. It was a horrifying thought.

Once Mike was satisfied that Mari and Jodi would be allowed to board their plane, he got down on his knees so he was eye level with Mari, who was visibly upset.

"No one will take you from your Mommy," he told Mari. "This will never happen to you again."

Jodi looked at Mari and didn't see any indication she was relaxing. Would she ever be able to trust adults again?

Their passports were stamped and they were allowed to continue to the gate.

Mike, not able to go any further with them, instructed Jodi not to talk to anyone while waiting for the plane. Jodi and Mari did as they were instructed and safely reached the gate and then boarded the plane.

Jodi carried on the fresh fruit she had purchased for Mari to eat, leaving her with just $70. They were seated three-quarters of the way back into coach, very near to where Jodi had sat when she traveled to Istanbul, just a few days before.

Jodi helped Mari get situated in their row where they were seated between two men.

Come on, get this plane in the air – I just want to get back to the U.S. where it is safe.

Jodi then understood why people would kiss the soil of their beloved country when they came back to the U.S.A.

"Are we going home?" Mari asked.

"Yes Sweetie, we are." What could Jodi say? She no longer had the home in Mari's memory. She knew she would have to explain to Mari about their new life. But there was time. She smiled at the little girl sitting next to her. Mari was munching on her fresh fruit and leaned on her mother's arm.

"Thank you for coming to get me," Mari said sweetly.

The plane finally lined up on the runway, accelerated and lifted off.

We made it Jodi thought. We're out of this nightmare.

Jodi smiled at Mari and they settled in for the 14-hour flight. Mari fell asleep and it gave Jodi time to think about what they were going to do. Frankly, she just didn't know. Yes, she imagined going back to her hometown and staying in her brother's cabin. She knew she had that option available to her. Yet, she knew that it was only a temporary solution. She looked down at Mari's little hand, still hanging on to hers so tight.

She had left $300 back at the cottage for when they got home, or if her parents needed to send it to her in Turkey. It was all that she had left. *What would they do? Where would they go?* For the first time in more than two years Jodi allowed herself to dream of their future. She looked again at Mari and she knew she had everything she needed.

CHAPTER 33

THURSDAY, AUG. 11, 2011
JFK AIRPORT, NEW YORK, NY
(BACK ON U.S. SOIL)

"WELCOME TO NEW YORK CITY." Jodi listened to the pilot's deep voice as she prepared to unbuckle her seat belt. She turned to assist Mari who was looking out over the seats through the window. At midday Eastern Time, the pavement looked like it was sizzling. Mari seemed fascinated by the carts rushing up to the plane's belly to retrieve cargo, their vehicles looking misshapen in the afternoon heat.

Jodi knew that the flight had been a bit delayed, landing later than expected. She wanted to make their connecting flight and didn't want to appear too nervous while waiting for the rows to empty out, one by one, in front of them.

The pilot announced that he had a special message. "Will Jodi Homaune please identify herself and her daughter before exiting the aircraft?"

Jodi froze. She dropped her gaze to see if Mari had heard the announcement. Sensing no change in her daughter, Jodi grabbed her briefcase, checked to see if Mari had her backpack and woodenly walked up the narrow aisle.

I can't believe I let my guard down and relaxed on the flight. Will they not even let me exit the plane? Why another hurdle?

Jodi instantly became alert, scrutinizing every person she could see. Why did the pilot want to know who she was? Had the Turkish government decided to file charges against her; did they know through Murat she had paid Kevin's attorney to work for them; did they know they had tricked Kevin into signing the paper to release Mari? Jodi was frantic. Her heart was beating through her chest and she leaned over to tell Mari to not let go of her hand and to stay close.

Within too short of a time, Jodi was at the entrance to the cockpit.

Bravely, but cautiously, she started to speak, squeezing her daughter's hand.

"I'm Jodi Homaune and this is my daugh …." Before she could complete her sentence, she and Mari were surrounded by six FBI agents.

"Hi Jodi, Robby sent us, we're here to help," said an agent looking straight into her eyes.

In the space of maybe three minutes, Jodi went from being horrified and unsure to relieved and feeling protected.

The agents quietly explained to Jodi that it was their job to get her to her connecting flight without interruption. She leaned over to Mari and placed a kiss on top of her head and told her quietly, "We are safe Sweetie, we are safe." Mari looked up and gave her mom a small smile.

As they walked, Jodi sensed something was wrong with Mari. Her hands had become extremely sweaty and when she looked at her daughter, Mari had turned deathly pale. She looked like she was going to pass out.

"Mari, what's wrong? Talk to Mommy," Jodi urged.

Mari was looking at the United States Flag.

"That flag is from where evil people come from," Mari said almost in a whisper.

Jodi was confused for a brief second and then realized what Mari was saying. "Mari," she started, "that is not an evil flag, and it is our Flag. The one we pledge allegiance to. Remember you learned it in kindergarten." Mari looked confused, but believed what her mother was saying.

"They hate that flag in Iran and they hate us and they hated me!"

Jodi quickly responded to her daughter's fear.

"No more worries, sweetie. That is a good flag with good people. You can trust Mommy."

Mari relaxed and smiled and Jodi watched her face returned to normal.

I can see pieces of our new journey to normal.

The group of eight, moved briskly to get to the gate of their connecting flight only to discover Jodi and Mari had missed it, because of the international flight delay. She was told that the FBI had authorized that she and Mari be put up in a hotel overnight. An agent named Shannon would escort them to the hotel and then pick them up the next morning. The airline had also provided Jodi and Mari with food vouchers.

While they were discussing what was going to happen, Mari said she had to go to the bathroom.

"I can take her," offered one of the female agents.

Jodi looked at her as if to say, "You've got to be kidding me." The agent immediately understood that Jodi wasn't going to let Mari out of her sight, so the three of them went into the nearest restroom in the busy terminal.

With $40 worth of food vouchers to use, Jodi and Mari picked out their food at the airport. Jodi was so relieved to be given the vouchers. She still had $70 get them back to Michigan. She made it fun by telling Mari that they were going to have a picnic in their hotel room and they would just get to relax.

Robby had called her and said he was aware of the changes and that he would call Matt and Nancy about the new plan that had them arriving home the following day. He told her he had provided them with Jodi and Mari's new flight information.

The agents were being very kind to Jodi and Mari. Some of them picked up their suitcases from baggage claim, so they could sit and rest. After the arrangements at the hotel were ready, they escorted them out to Agent Shannon's vehicle and she drove them to the hotel. Shannon checked them in and led mother and daughter to their room. Jodi hadn't taken the time to look at all of the agent's cards at the airport and didn't know Shannon's role with the FBI; if she was a victim's specialist like Donna, or an agent like Robby.

Jodi felt safe when Shannon opened the door and scanned the room before they entered. She told Jodi that she would be at their door in the morning to pick them up to take them back to the airport.

"Enjoy your evening. I'll see you both soon," said Shannon. She leaned down and looked directly at Mari.

"Welcome back to the United States Mari, we missed you." Mari looked up at Shannon, her face glowing with happiness.

Alone once again, mother and daughter spread their sandwiches, chips and bottled water out on the bed on towels Jodi had arranged picnic style.

Shortly after eating, Mari fell asleep, exhausted. Jodi on the other hand, was wide awake, still marveling at the miracle of having her daughter back.

She made a quick phone call to Donna and asked her to please call her family and let them know they were OK, she explained she just needed a moment to herself to gather her thoughts.

Jodi lay next to Mari, even though there were two queen beds in the room. She stroked Mari's hair and gave her a kiss on her head. She leaned back against the pillows and just stared up at the ceiling and started talking to God.

"Dear Lord, thank you for all you do in this world. Thank you for handling all of this to bring Mari and me back together again. I promise I will forever spend my days helping others find their missing loved ones. No one should have to do this or go through this to be with the ones they love. Thank you – Amen."

She lay there continuing to stare at the ceiling and thought about the FBI and about how overwhelmed she was at the kindness of all of the FBI agents who had worked with her. She thought about how Shannon's words earlier in the night had affected Mari. Shannon didn't know them and most likely knew very little about their story. It touched Jodi to hear her welcome Mari back to the United States and to tell her she was missed. Jodi thought the words came naturally to the agent, but the impact of what she said was absolutely inspired. Robby and Donna kept crossing Jodi's mind as she stared at the ceiling, listening to Mari breathe.

Without the help of the FBI she wouldn't have her daughter again. Before working so personally with the agency, she had a perception that they captured criminals and worked on crimes which local and state police didn't handle. She knew very little about the FBI, except one of her father's students, after a long career as a detective, went on to work for the FBI. She thought the random thoughts which were popping into her mind, were funny to think about, with everything else going on and Mari by her side.

What would she have done without Robby and Donna? The agents were her link to Mari. She lay on the bed and thought about what all three of them had been through and how she could never thank them enough.

How do you say "thank you" to someone who helped bring the one person you love more than life back to you?

"I am sure Robby and Donna were just doing their jobs in their roles as FBI agents, but they were so much more to me in my journey to get Mari home. I knew God had blessed me with them," Jodi silently thought.

She also thought about all the people and agencies who would want to take credit for Mari's rescue. But Jodi credited the FBI as playing the primary role.

"The FBI - what an incredible organization that took the time to help rescue one little girl held in Iran."

To the world she is just one little girl, but to me she is my world and thanks to the FBI my world was back home.

For a brief moment Jodi's thoughts turned to Kevin. She was certain by that time, he had figured out Mari was out of the orphanage and out of Turkey. For a brief second she actually felt sorry for him that he would never see his daughter again; however, the moment passed and

Jodi saw that it was 5:30 in the morning and she had spent all night with her thoughts.

She was in New York City with her daughter by her side and together they were starting a new chapter in their lives.

CHAPTER 34

FRIDAY, AUG. 12, 2011
NEW YORK TO MICHIGAN

A SOFT KNOCK ON THE door let Jodi know that Shannon was outside their door, ready to pick them up. Jodi looked through the peep hole to just make sure, and then opened the door to let her in.

Shannon asked how their night had been and asked Mari how she enjoyed her picnic and if she slept well. Mari nodded and smiled but was busy packing her little toys into her bag.

Jodi was filled with excitement knowing they would soon be leaving New York for Detroit. They were finally going home!

Because she hadn't slept much in the past two weeks, Jodi was a little confused about the day.

"I have a silly question to ask you Shannon," she said. Shannon looked at her with an expression that encouraged Jodi to go ahead and ask her anything she wanted.

"What day is it?" Jodi knew her phone said it was Aug. 13, but she didn't know what day of the week it was.

Shannon kind of laughed and answered.

"Don't worry, it's Saturday. You have been going full force and with traveling so many hours and the time change, it's really a normal question to ask."

When they arrived at the airport, another agent joined them and they accompanied Jodi and Mari through security, down the concourse and to the gate where both agents waited with them until they boarded the plane.

They had a 45-minute wait before boarding, so Mari and Jodi sat with the agents and just chit-chatted.

The agents were aware of their story, but didn't know any details, Jodi learned. They talked with Mari and told her they had heard of her and that they thought she was a brave little girl. Mari giggled in response and held on tight to her mother while sitting on her lap.

Mari was very excited as Jodi had told her that after they were picked up from the airport in Michigan, they would be traveling to see her grandparents. Mari said she remembered them, but didn't remember what they looked like. Jodi showed her their pictures again, which caused Mari to smile.

There had been no opportunity to shop and no extra money anyway so Mari was wearing the same skirt she had on the day before, with Jodi's tank top and Jodi's white sweater. She still was wearing her mother's sandals. In spite of it, Jodi felt as if they looked like two ordinary travelers. Who would ever believe the journey the two of them had just completed? She looked around at the people waiting for the plane with a renewed sense of curiosity about her fellow travelers and what they were experiencing in their lives.

The gate agent announced it was time to board. Again, checking to make sure they had all their bags, Jodi and Mari got in line to board their plane. As they went through the check-point, they turned to see the two agents waving goodbye. Jodi hoped that they knew how much she appreciated what they had done for them.

The plane landed at Detroit Metro at approximately 11:30 a.m. Jodi wondered if she would see more FBI agents when they stepped off the plane but no one seemed to be looking for her or trying to get her attention. She held tight to Mari's hand and walked off the plane. She held her head up, scanning the gate waiting area for anyone she knew. Not a sign of anyone and it felt wonderful!

She walked up the concourse and as soon as she and Mari were on the escalator, she dialed Robby.

"We did it!" Jodi squealed when she heard him answer.

"Where are you Jodi?" Robby said, not sounding excited for her at all.

"On the escalator," Jodi said confidently.

"Are there FBI agents around you?" Robby asked.

"No, should there be?"

"Yes," he answered.

"But Robby, we're fine," Jodi insisted, as she and Mari stepped off the escalator and started walking toward the baggage claim. Jodi had a new bounce to her walk. It was a movement of complete joy at having her daughter holding her hand. She knew there was much more Mari was going to tell her and she was prepared for the unknown, but she was incredibly happy.

As she neared the baggage carousel she looked around for Matt. She knew he would be there. She turned and there he was, standing nearby, accompanied by his family. There they were: Matt, Nancy, Luke and Jake, just like when she had left them six days ago.

The look in her brother's eyes made her want to cry, but she didn't. Matt rushed to his sister and gave her a big bear hug before leaning down to ask Mari if he could hug her.

"Yes," she answered her uncle shyly. Jodi could hear Matt's sigh of relief as he embraced his niece.

Nancy, always thinking ahead, handed Mari two balloons. One said "Welcome Home Mari!" which quickly escaped Mari's hand and floated very high to the ceiling. Jodi tied the other around Mari's wrist, which made her smile as she reached up to give her aunt a hug. Mari smiled as she turned to her cousins.

Jodi could see her beginning to recognize Luke and Jake. It seemed that time slowed down as her young cousins gave Mari time to recognize them. It was the first of many moments in a long time that Jodi didn't mind having time move at its own pace.

Their happy reunion was joined by two FBI agents who introduced themselves and told Jodi that Robby had sent them to make sure that they were OK, welcome Mari and Jodi back and to make sure they had a ride home.

Jodi introduced her family to them and thanked the agents for coming. They gave Jodi their cards and told her that if she or Mari needed anything to give them a call.

After their luggage arrived, the family boarded Matt and Nancy's van. Mari and Jodi sat side-by-side in the back seat with Mari asking her mom a "million" questions. Jodi's little chatterbox had returned.

Matt looked back in his mirror, locked eyes with his sister and smiled. His sister had done what she set out to do; bring her daughter home.

Epilogue

For the two years and three months that Mari was held in Iran, Jodi was allowed to speak to her daughter for a total of two hours and eight minutes. She later learned the lack of contact with Mari and the monitoring of the conversations were because Kevin was afraid that Mari would tell Jodi about the beatings and abuse she was suffering at his hands.

Kevin Homaune was captured in Germany on May 20, 2012, when German officials detained him, having taken notice of the red Interpol warning on him. The United States sought extradition the next day. Around June 28, the custody of Kevin was transferred to the U.S. Marshals Service in Germany.

Kevin Hussain Homaune pleaded guilty to charges of International Parental Kidnapping on Oct. 25, 2012 and was banned from the United States for 10 years. He was removed to Canada on December 23, 2012. He was also ordered to pay financial restitution to Jodi of more than $119,500, an order which lasts 20 years. To this day, he has not paid any of the amount.

For two years and three months Jodi had worked with the FBI, the State Department, the Swiss Embassy in Tehran, Iran, the American Embassy in Warsaw, Poland, The National Center for Missing and Exploited Children, her attorneys and anyone else who would listen.

It worked.

Because of her experiences, Jodi with her daughter established The MotherDaughter Fund (The MD Fund) in 2012. The MD Fund is a resource for families to lean on during their journey to find their loved ones and is a strong "helping hand" during recovery and reunification.

Along with Jodi, The MD Fund boasts a growing team of volunteers with respective expertise who assist in various service areas including investigation, reunification, project management, and fundraising.

Moving forward, The MD Fund plans to develop a support group for individuals who have experienced the loss and recovery of their loved ones and are in the process of healing.

Jodi should know what it takes; she's been there and back.

Jodi also volunteers for Team Hope of the National Center for Missing and Exploited Children.

Made in the USA
Lexington, KY
10 September 2016